PRACTICAL
ARGUMENTATION

BY

GEORGE K. PATTEE, A.M.

Assistant Professor of English and Rhetoric in The Pennsylvania
State College

NEW YORK

THE CENTURY CO.

1909

J. F. TAPLEY CO.
New York

PRACTICAL ARGUMENTATION

TO

FRED LEWIS PATTEE

Preface

THE author's aim has been to produce a book that is practical,—practical from the student's standpoint, and practical from the teacher's standpoint. The study of Argumentation has often been criticized for being purely academic, or for being a mere stepping-stone to the study of law. It has even been said that courses in Argumentation and Debate have been introduced into American colleges and universities for no other purpose than to give the intellectual student the opportunity, so long monopolized by his athletic classmate, to take part in intercollegiate contests. The purpose of this book is to teach Argumentation, which is not a science by itself but one of the four branches of Rhetoric, in such a way as to remove these criticisms.

Largely by his choice of illustrative material the author has endeavored to show that this subject is confined neither to the class room nor to any one profession. He has drawn his illustrations, for the most part, from contemporary and popular sources; he has had recourse to many current magazines, newspapers, books, and recent speeches, hoping to show thereby that Argumentation is a practical subject. On the other hand, he has carefully avoided taking a majority of his illustrations either from students' work or from legal practice, criminal cases especially being seldom used on the ground that although they afford the easiest examples a writer can give, they

Preface

furnish the least help to the average student, who, unless he studies law, will rarely, perhaps never, have occasion to argue upon such subjects.

This book cannot justly be called the effort of a single author. It is rather an outgrowth of the work that for many years has been carried on by the English department at The Pennsylvania State College. The book has, in fact, gradually developed in the class room. Every rule that is given has been tested time and again; every step has been carefully thought out and taught for several years.

The author wishes to acknowledge especial indebtedness to Professor Fred Lewis Pattee, who both inspired the writing of the book and assisted in the work. To Professor A. Howry Espenshade are due many thanks for invaluable suggestions and advice, and for a careful reading of the greater part of the manuscript. Mr. William S. Dye is also to be thanked for valuable assistance. As a student the author studied Baker's *Principles of Argumentation;* as a teacher he has taught Laycock and Scales' *Argumentation and Debate*, Alden's *The Art of Debate*, and Foster's *Argumentation and Debating*. The debt he owes to these is beyond estimate.

STATE COLLEGE, PA.
March 17, 1909

Contents

Appendix.

ix

PRACTICAL ARGUMENTATION

PRACTICAL ARGUMENTATION

CHAPTER I

PRELIMINARIES

ARGUMENTATION is the art of presenting truth so that others will accept it and act in accordance with it. Debate is a special form of argumentation: it is oral argumentation carried on by opposing sides.

A consideration of the service which argumentation performs shows that it is one of the noblest and most useful of arts. By argumentation men overthrow error and discover truth. Courts of law, deliberative assemblies, and all bodies of people that engage in discussion recognize this fact. Argumentation threshes out a problem until the chaff has blown away, when it is easy to see just what kernels of truth remain and what action ought to be taken. Men of affairs, before entering upon any great enterprise, call in advocates of different systems, and

Preliminaries

by becoming familiar with arguments from every point of view try to discover what is best. This method of procedure presupposes a difference of opinion and belief among men, and holds that when each one tries to establish his ideas, the truth will remain, and that which is false will be swept away.

The field of argumentation includes every kind of discourse that attempts to change man's actions or opinions. Exposition is explanation when only one theory or one interpretation of the facts is possible; when views of truth or of policy conflict, and one course is expounded in opposition to another, the process becomes argumentation. This art is used not only by professional speakers, but by men of every occupation. The schoolboy pleading for a holiday, the workman seeking employment, the statesman advocating a principle of government are all engaged in some form of argumentation. Everywhere that men meet together, on the street or in the assembly hall, debate is certain to arise. Written argument is no less common. Hardly a periodical is published but contains argumentative writing. The fiery editorial that urges voters to the polls, the calm and polished essay that points out the dangers of organized labor, the scientific

4

Preliminaries

treatise that demonstrates the practicability of a sea-level canal on the Isthmus are attempts to change existing conditions and ideas, and thus come within the field of argumentation.

The practical benefit to be derived from the study and application of the principles of argumentation can hardly be overestimated. The man who wishes to influence the opinions and actions of others, who wishes to become a leader of men in however great or however humble a sphere, must be familiar with this art. The editor, the lawyer, the merchant, the contractor, the laborer — men in every walk of life — depend for their success upon bringing others to believe, in certain instances, as they believe. Everywhere men who can point out what is right and best, and can bring others to see it and act upon it, win the day. Another benefit to be obtained from the study of argumentation is the ability to be convinced intelligently. The good arguer is not likely to be carried away by specious arguments or fallacious reasoning. He can weigh every bit of evidence; he can test the strength and weakness of every statement; he can separate the essential from the unessential; and he can distinguish between prejudice and reason. A master of the art of argumentation can both present his case convincingly to others, and discover the truth in a matter that is presented to him.

Argumentation can hardly be considered as a distinct art standing by itself; it is rather a composite of several arts, deriving its fundamentals from them, and depending upon them for its existence. In the first place, since argumentation is spoken or written discourse, it belongs to rhetoric, and the rules which govern composition apply to it as strongly as to any other kind of expression. In fact, perhaps rhetorical principles should be observed in argumentation more rigidly than elsewhere, for in the case of narration, description, or exposition, the reader or hearer, in an endeavor to derive pleasure or profit, is seeking the author, while in argumentation it is the author who is trying to force his ideas upon the audience. Hence an argument must contain nothing crude or repulsive, but must be attractive in every detail. In the second place, any composition that attempts to alter beliefs must deal with reasons, and the science of reasoning is logic. There is no need for the student of argumentation to make an exhaustive study of this science, for the good arguer is not obliged to know all the different ways the mind may work; he must, how-

Preliminaries

ever, know how it should work in order to produce trustworthy results, and to the extent of teaching correct reasoning, argumentation includes logic. In the third place, a study of the emotions belongs to argumentation. According to the definition, argumentation aims both at presenting truth and compelling action. As action depends to a great extent upon man's emotions, the way to arouse his feelings and passions is a fundamental principle of this art.

Argumentation, then, which is commonly classified as the fourth division of rhetoric, consists of two fundamental elements. The part that is based upon logic and depends for its effectiveness upon pure reasoning is called *conviction;* the part that consists of an emotional appeal to the people addressed is called *persuasion.* If the only purpose of argumentation were to demonstrate the truth or falsity of a hypothesis, conviction alone would be sufficient. But its purpose is greater than this: it aims both (1) to convince men that certain ideas are true, and also (2) to persuade them to act in accordance with the truth presented. Neither conviction nor persuasion can with safety be omitted. An appeal to the intellect alone may demonstrate principles that cannot be refuted; it may prove beyond a doubt that certain theories are logical and right, and ought to be accepted. But this sort of argument is likely to leave the person addressed cold and unmoved and unwilling to give up his former ideas and practices. A purely intellectual discourse upon the evils resulting from a high tariff would scarcely cause a life-long protectionist to change his politics. If, however, some emotion such as duty, public spirit, or patriotism were aroused, the desired action might result. Again it frequently happens that before the arguer can make any appeal to the logical faculties of those he wishes to influence, he will first have to use persuasion in order to gain their attention and to arouse their interest either in himself or in his subject. On the other hand, persuasion alone is undoubtedly of even less value than conviction alone. A purely persuasive argument can never be trusted to produce lasting effects. As soon as the emotions have cooled, if no reasonable conviction remains to guide future thought and action, the plea that at first seemed so powerful is likely to be forgotten. The preacher whose sermons are all persuasion may, for a time, have many converts, but it will take something besides emotional ecstasy to keep them " in good and regular standing."

The proportion of conviction and persuasion to

Preliminaries

be used in any argumentative effort depends entirely upon the attending circumstances. If the readers or hearers possess a high degree of intelligence and education, conviction should predominate; for it is a generally accepted fact that the higher man rises in the scale of civilization, the less he is moved by emotion. A lawyer's argument before a judge contains little except reasoning; before a jury persuasion plays an important part. In the next place, the arguer must consider the attitude of those whom he would move. If they are favorably disposed, he may devote most of his time to reasoning; if they are hostile, he must use more persuasion. Also the correct proportion varies to some extent according to the amount of action desired. In an intercollegiate debate where little or no action is expected to result, persuasion may almost be neglected; but the political speech or editorial that urges men to follow its instructions usually contains at least as much persuasion as conviction.

The aspirant for distinction in argumentation should study and acquire certain characteristics common to all good arguers. First of all, he should strive to gain the ability to analyze. No satisfactory discussion can ever take place until the contestants have picked the question to pieces and discovered just exactly what it means. The man who does not analyze his subject is likely to seize upon ideas that are merely connected with it, and fail to find just what is involved by the question as a whole. The man skillful in argumentation, however, considers each word of the proposition in the light of its definition, and only after much thought and study decides that he has found the real meaning of the question. But the work of analysis does not end here; every bit of proof connected with the case must be analyzed that its value and its relation to the matter in hand may be determined. Many an argument is filled with what its author thought was proof, but what, upon close inspection, turns out to be mere assertion or fallacious reasoning. This error is surpassed only by the fault of bringing in as proof that which has no direct bearing at all upon the question at issue. Furthermore, the arguer must analyze not only his own side of the discussion but also the work of his opponent, so that with a full knowledge of what is strong and what is weak he may make his attack to the best advantage. Next to the ability to analyze, the most important qualification for an arguer to possess is the faculty of clearly presenting his case. New ideas, new truths are seldom readily ac-

cepted, and it is never safe to assume that the hearer
or the reader of an argument will laboriously work
his way through a mass of obscure reasoning. Absolute clearness of expression is essential. The
method of arriving at a conclusion should be so plain
that no one can avoid seeing what is proved and how
it is proved. Lincoln's great success as a debater
was due largely to his clearness of presentation. In
the third place, the person who would control his
fellow men must assume qualities of leadership.
Remembering that men can be led, but seldom be
driven, he must show his audience how he himself
has reached certain conclusions, and then by leading
them along the same paths of reasoning, bring them
to the desired destination. If exhortation, counsel,
and encouragement are required, they must be at
his command. Moreover, a leader who wishes to
attract followers must be earnest and enthusiastic.
The least touch of insincerity or indifference will
ruin all. To analyze ideas, to present them clearly,
and as a leader to enforce them enthusiastically and
sincerely are necessary qualities for every arguer.

A debater should possess additional attainments.
He ought to be a ready thinker. The disputant
who depends entirely upon a set speech is greatly
handicapped. Since it is impossible to tell before-

Preliminaries

hand just what arguments an opponent will use and what line of attack he will pursue, the man who cannot mass his forces to meet the requirements of the minute is at great disadvantage. Of course all facts and ideas must be mastered beforehand, but unless one is to be the first speaker, he can most effectually determine during the progress of the debate just what arguments are preferable and what their arrangement should be. A debater must also have some ability as a speaker. He need not be graceful or especially fluent, though these accomplishments are of service, but he must be forceful. Not only his words, but also his manner must reveal the earnestness and enthusiasm he feels. His argument, clear, irrefutable, and to the point, should go forth in simple, burning words that enter into the hearts and understanding of his hearers.

CHAPTER II

THE SUBJECT

THE subject of an argument must always be a complete statement. The reason for this requirement lies in the fact that an argument can occur only when men have conflicting opinions about a certain thought, and try to prove the truth or falsity of this definite idea. Since a *term* — a word, phrase, or other combination of words not a complete sentence — suggests many ideas, but never stands for one particular idea, it is absurd as a subject to be argued. A debatable subject is always a *proposition,* a statement in which something is affirmed or denied. It would be impossible to uphold or attack the mere term, " government railroad supervision," for this expression carries with it no specific thought. It may suggest that government railroad supervision has been inadequate in the past; or that government supervision is at present unnecessary; or that the government is about to assume stricter supervision. The term affords no

13

The Subject

common ground on which the contestants would have to meet. If, however, some exact idea were expressed in such a statement as, " Further government railroad supervision is necessary for the best interests of the United States," an argument might well follow.

Although the subject of an argument must be a complete thought, it does not follow that this proposition is always explicitly stated or formulated in words. The same distinction between subject and title that exists in other kinds of writing is found also in argumentation; the subject is a statement of the matter about which the controversy centers; the title is the name by which the composition is known. Sometimes the subject serves as the title, and sometimes the subject is left to be discovered in the body of the work. The title of the speech delivered by Webster in the Senate, January 26, 1830, is " Webster's Reply to Hayne "; the subject, in the form of a resolution, is found close to the opening sentences :—

Resolved, That the Committee on Public Lands be instructed to inquire and report the quantity of public lands remaining unsold within each State and Territory, and whether it be expedient to limit for a certain period the sales of the public lands to such lands only as have

The Subject

heretofore been offered for sale, and are now subject to entry at the minium price. And, also, whether the office of Surveyor-General, and some of the land offices, may not be abolished without detriment to the public interest; or whether it be expedient to adopt measures to hasten the sales and extend more rapidly the surveys of the public lands.

The thirteen resolutions offered by Burke form the subject of the argument known by the title, " Burke's Speech on Conciliation with America." A recent issue of *The Outlook* contained an article entitled " Russian Despotism "; careful reading disclosed that the subject was this, " The Present Government of Russia has no Right to Exist." In legislative proceedings the subject of argument is found in the form of a bill, or a motion, or a resolution; in law courts it is embodied in statements called " pleadings," which " set forth with certainty and with truth the matters of fact or of law, the truth or falsity of which must be decided to decide the case." [1] In college debate it is customary to frame the subject in the form of a resolution, and to use this resolution as the title. The generally accepted form is as follows:

Resolved, That the United States army should be permanently enlarged.

[1] Laycock and Scales' Argumentation and Debate, page.

The Subject

Notice the use of italics, of punctuation marks, and of capital letters.

In all kinds of argumentation, whether the proposition to be discussed is clearly expressed or not, the arguer must keep his subject constantly in mind, that his efforts may all be directed toward a definite end in view — to convince and persuade his audience. In debate the speaker should plainly state the subject, and constantly hold it up to the attention of the audience. This procedure renders it impossible for an opponent to ignore the question and evade the real issue.

Only those who are debating for practice experience any difficulty in obtaining a subject. In the business world men argue because they are confronted with some perplexing problem, because some issue arises that demands discussion; but the student, generally speaking, chooses his own topic. Therefore a few suggestions in regard to the choice of a subject and the wording of a proposition are likely to be of considerable service to him.

The student should first select some general, popular topic of the day in which he is interested. He uld, for several reasons, not the least of which he will thus gain considerable information be of value to him outside the class room, select a popular topic rather than one that has been worn out or that is comparatively unknown. He should, moreover, choose an interesting topic, for then his work will be more agreeable and consequently of a higher order. Of this general idea he must decide upon some specific phase which readily lends itself to discussion. Then he has to express this specific idea in the form of a proposition. As it is not always an easy matter to state a proposition with precision and fairness, he must take this last step very cautiously. One must always exercise great care in choosing words that denote the exact meaning he wishes to convey. Many writers and speakers have found themselves in false positions just because, upon examination, it was found that their subjects did not express the precise meaning that was intended.

Moreover, in phrasing the proposition, the debater should so state the subject that the affirmative side, the side that opens the discussion, is the one to advocate a change in existing conditions or belief. This method obviously corresponds to the way in which business is conducted in practical affairs. No one has reason to defend an established condition until it is first attacked. The law presumes a man to be innocent until he is proved guilty, and there-

The Subject

fore it is the prosecution, the side to affirm guilt, that opens the case. The question about government ownership of railroads should be so worded that the affirmative side will advocate the new system, and the negative will uphold the old. It should be stated thus: "*Resolved,* That all railroads in the United States should be owned and operated by the Federal government." This obligation of adducing evidence and reasoning to support one side of a proposition before an answer from the other side can be demanded, is called *burden of proof.* The "burden" always rests upon the side that advocates a change, and the proposition should be so worded that the affirmative will have to undertake this duty.

One more principle must be observed: nothing in the wording of the subject should give one side any advantage over the other. Argument can exist only when reasonable men have a difference of opinion. If the wording of the proposition removes this difference, no discussion can ensue. For instance, the word "undesirable," if allowed to stand in the following proposition, precludes any debate: "*Resolved,* That all colleges should abolish the undesirable game of football."

From the preceding suggestions it is seen that

The Subject

the subject of an argument is a definite, restricted thought derived from some general idea. Whether expressed or not, the subject must be a proposition, not a term. In debate the proposition is usually framed in the form of a resolution. This resolution must always be so worded that the burden of proof will rest upon the affirmative side. Nothing in the wording of the proposition should give either side any advantage over the other. These principles have to do with the manner of expression; subjects will next be considered with respect to the ideas they contain.

A common and convenient method of classification divides propositions into two groups: propositions of policy, and propositions of fact. The first class consists of those propositions that aim to prove the truth of a theory, that indicate a preference for a certain policy, for a certain method of action. The second class comprises those propositions that affirm or deny the occurrence of an event, or the existence of a fact. Propositions of policy usually, though not always, contain the word *should* or *ought;* propositions of fact usually contain some form of the word *to be.* The following illustrations will make the distinction plainer:—

The Subject

Propositions of Policy.

The United States should adopt a system of bounties and subsidies for the protection of the American merchant marine.

State laws prohibiting secular employment on Sunday should be repealed.

A city furnishes a more desirable location for a college than the country.

The aggressions of England in Africa are justifiable.

Propositions of Fact.

Homer wrote the Iliad.

Nero was guilty of burning Rome.

Mary, Queen of Scots, murdered her husband.

The most convenient method of studying propositions to see what subjects are desirable for student debates is to consider first those propositions that should be avoided.

1. **Propositions with only one side.** As argumentation presupposes a difference of opinion about a certain subject, evidently it is impossible to argue upon a subject on which all are agreed. Sometimes such propositions as, " *Resolved,* That

The Subject

Napoleon was a great soldier," and "*Resolved,*
That railroads should take every precaution to protect the lives of their passengers," are found on the
programs of literary societies and debating clubs.
In such cases mere comment, not debate, can follow.
Only subjects on which reasonable men actually disagree are suitable for argument.

2. **Ambiguous propositions.** If a proposition
is capable of several interpretations, those who
choose it as a subject for an argument are liable not
to agree on what it means, and one side will debate
in accordance with one interpretation, and the other
side in accordance with a totally different interpretation. Thus the opponents will never meet in conflict except when they explain their subject. For
example, in a certain debate on the question, "*Resolved,* That colleges should abolish all athletic
sports," the affirmative held that only interclass and
intercollegiate games were involved; while the negative maintained that the term " athletic sports " included all forms of athletic games participated in by
college men. Manifestly the debate hinged largely
on the definition of this term; but as there was no
authority to settle just what was meant, the debate
was a failure. It is usually desirable, and frequently
necessary, to explain what the subject means, for un-

less it has some meaning which both sides are bound to accept, the argument becomes a mere controversy over the definition of words. Another ambiguous proposition would be, " Republican government in the United States is preferable to any other." The word " republican " is open to two legitimate definitions, and since the context does not explain which meaning is intended, a debater is at liberty to accept either definition that he wishes. A few alterations easily turn this proposition into a debatable subject, " Government by the Republican party in the United States is preferable to any other."

3. **Too general propositions.** It is never wise for a writer or a speaker to choose a subject which is so general or so abstract that he cannot handle it with some degree of completeness and facility. Not only will such work be difficult and distasteful to him, but it will be equally distasteful and uninteresting to his audience. No student can write good themes on such subjects as, " War," " The Power of the Press," " Race Prejudice "; nor can he argue well on propositions like, " *Resolved,* That wars are justifiable "; " *Resolved,* That the pen is mightier than the sword "; or " *Resolved,* That race prejudice is justifiable." These are entirely beyond his scope. But he can handle restricted propositions

The Subject

that have to do with one phase of some concrete, tangible event or idea. "*Resolved,* That Japan was justified in waging war against Russia"; "*Resolved,* That Bacon wrote the plays commonly attributed to Shakespeare"; "*Resolved,* That the segregation of Japanese school children in San Francisco is for the best interests of all concerned," are subjects that can be argued with success.

4. Combined propositions. It sometimes happens that several heterogeneous ideas, each of which by itself would form an excellent subject for argument, are embodied in a single proposition. The difficulty of arguing on this kind of subject is apparent. It is none too easy to establish one idea satisfactorily; but when several ideas must be upheld and defended, the work is enormous and sometimes open to the charge of inconsistency. Moreover, the principle of Unity demands that a composition be about a single topic. The proposition, "*Resolved,* That Aaron Burr was guilty of murder and should have been put to death," involves two debatable subjects, each of which is of sufficient importance to stand in a proposition by itself: "Was Burr guilty of murder?" and "Should a murderer be punished by death?" The error of combining in a compound sentence several distinct subjects for debate is generally detected with ease; but when the error of combination exists in a simple sentence, it is not always so obvious. In the case of the subject, " *Resolved,* That foreign immigrants have been unjustly treated by the United States," there are, as the same privileges have not been granted all immigrants, several debatable questions. One who attempts to argue on this subject must take into consideration the treatment that has been accorded the Chinese, the English, the Germans, the Italians, the paupers, the well-to-do, and others. In one case the laws may be palpably unfair, and in another case, all that can be desired.

When two ideas, however, are very closely related and are dependent upon each other for interpretation and support, they may and sometimes should be combined in the same proposition. For example, " Education should be compulsory to the age of sixteen," involves two main issues: " Education should be compulsory," and " The age of sixteen is the proper limit." But in this case the one who advocates compulsory education is under obligation to explain some definite system, and this explanation must include the establishing of some limit. To name this limit in the proposition renders the argument clearer to an audience and fairer to an

The Subject

opponent. For similar reasons, the proposition, " The Federal government should own and operate the railroads in the United States," cannot be condemned on the ground that it is a proposition with more than one main issue.

Propositions, then, adapted to class room argument, are those which give rise to a conflict of opinion; which contain a definite and unmistakable thought; which are specific and sufficiently restricted to admit of thorough treatment; and which contain a single idea.

Furthermore, the student will do well to select subjects that are as nearly as possible like the problems which statesmen, educators, professional and business men meet in practical life. He should try to remove his argument as far as he can from the realm of pure academic exercise, and endeavor to gain some insight into the issues that are now confronting the makers of modern civilization. The student who takes this work seriously is sure to gain information, form opinions, and acquire habits of thought that will be of great practical value to him when he takes his place as a man among men.

EXERCISES

A. Narrow each of the following terms into good, debatable propositions : —

The Subject

Election of Senators; Chinese exclusion; woman suffrage; temperance; compulsory manual training; the honor system; compulsory education; vivisection; reciprocity; an enlarged army; the educational voting test; strikes; bounties and subsidies; capital punishment; Hamlet's insanity; municipal government; permanent copyright; athletics; civil service; military training; Panama canal; jury system; foreign acquisitions; Monroe Doctrine; forest reserves; protective tariff.

B. Criticise the following propositions:—

1. The existence and attributes of the Supreme Being can be proved without the aid of divine revelation.

2. More money is spent for luxuries than for necessities.

3. The growth of large fortunes should be checked by a graduated income tax and an inheritance tax.

4. The Monroe Doctrine should receive the support of every American.

5. Hard work is the secret of success.

6. Law is a better profession than medicine.

7. College football should be abolished and lacrosse adopted in its place.

8. Newspapers exert a powerful influence on modern politics.

9. The United States postal system should be under the control of the Federal government.

10. The shortest distance between two points is a straight line.

11. Immigration is detrimental to the United States.

12. President ——'s foreign policy should be upheld.

13. Canada should not be annexed to the United States.

14. The cruel banishment of the Acadians was unjust.

15. Beauty has practical uses.

16. The democratic policy of government would be for the best interests of the Philippines.

26

The Subject

17. Dicken's novels, which are superior to Scott's, effected reforms.

18. An unconstitutional income tax should not be levied.

19. A majority vote of a jury should not convict or acquit.

20. Edison is a great inventor.

CHAPTER III

THE INTRODUCTION — PERSUASION

Every complete argument consists of three parts: introduction, discussion, and conclusion. Each of these divisions has definite and specific duties to perform. The work of the introduction is three-fold: (1) to conciliate the audience; (2) to explain the subject; and (3) to outline the discussion. As the conciliation of the audience is accomplished by an appeal to the emotions rather than to the reason, it is properly classified under persuasion. Explaining the proposition and outlining the discussion are of an expository nature and will be discussed under the head of conviction.

As has been stated in a previous chapter, the amount of persuasion to be used in any piece of argumentative work depends entirely upon the attending circumstances. The subject, audience, author, occasion, and purpose of the effort must be taken into consideration. But whether the amount used be great or small, practically every argument

Persuasion in the Introduction

should begin with conciliation. The conciliation of
the audience — the word *audience* is used throughout this book to designate both hearers and readers
— consists of gaining the good will of those to be
convinced, of arousing their interest, and of rendering them open to conviction. No argument can be
expected to attain any considerable degree of success so long as anything about its author, or anything
in the subject itself, is peculiarly disagreeable to the
people it is designed to affect. If the ill will remains too great, it is not likely that the argument
will ever reach those for whom it is intended, much
less produce the desired result. In addressing
Southern sympathizers at Liverpool, during the
Civil War, Beecher had to fight even for a hearing.
The speech of an unpopular Senator frequently
empties the Senate chamber. Men of one political
belief often refuse to read the publications of the
opposite party. Obviously, the first duty of the
introduction is to gain the approval of the audience.
In the next place, interest must be aroused. Active
dislike is less frequently encountered than indifference. How many times sermons, lectures, books
have failed in their object just because no one took
any interest in them! There was no opposition, no
hostility; every one wished the cause well; and yet

the effort failed to meet with any attention or response. The argument did not arouse interest — and interest is a prime cause of attention and of action. In the third place, the conciliatory part of the introduction should induce the audience to assume an unbiased, judicial attitude, ready to decide the question according to the strength of the proof. This result is not always easy of attainment. Longstanding beliefs, prejudice, stubbornness must be overcome, and a desire for the truth substituted for everything else. All this is frequently difficult, but unless an arguer can gain the good will of the people addressed, arouse their interest, and render them willing to be convinced, no amount of reasoning is likely to produce much effect.

Now the question arises, How is it possible to conciliate the audience? To this query there is no answer that will positively guarantee success. The arguer must always study his audience and suit his discourse to the occasion. What means success in one instance may bring failure in another. The secret of the whole matter is adaptability. Humor, gravity, pathos, even defiance may at times be used to advantage. It is not always possible, however, for the orator or writer to know beforehand just the kind of people he is to address. In this case

Persuasion in the Introduction

it is usually best for him to follow out a few well
established principles that most arguers have found
to be of benefit.

Modesty. Modesty in word and action is indispensable to one who would gain the friendship of
his audience. Anything that savors of egotism at
once creates a feeling of enmity. No one can endure another's consciousness of superiority even
though the superiority be real. An appearance of
haughtiness, self-esteem, condescension, intolerance
of inferiors, or a desire for personal glory will at
once raise barriers of dislike. On the other hand,
modesty should never be carried so far as to become
affectation; that attitude is equally despicable. Personal unobtrusiveness should exist without being
conspicuous. *The arguer should always take the
attitude that the cause he is upholding is greater
than its advocate.*

In the following quotations, compare the over-
bearing arrogance of Burke's introduction with the
simple modesty of Proctor's:—

Mr. Speaker, I rise under some embarrassment occa-
sioned by a feeling of delicacy toward one-half of the
house, and of sovereign contempt for the other half.[1]

Mr. President, more importance seems to be attached
by others to my recent visit to Cuba than I had given it,

[1] Edmund Burke, House of Commons, March 22, 1775.

Persuasion in the Introduction

and it has been suggested that I make a public statement of what I saw and how the situation impressed me. This I do on account of the public interest in all that concerns Cuba, and to correct some inaccuracies that have, not unnaturally, appeared in reported interviews with me.[1]

Fairness. Few things will assist an arguer more in securing a respectful hearing from those who do not agree with him, but whom he would convince, than the quality of fairness. The arguer should take the position of one seeking the truth regardless of what it may be. If he wishes others to look at the question from his standpoint, he will have to show that he is willing to consider the question from their point of view. Everything in the shape of prejudice, everything which would tend to indicate that he had formed conclusions prior to his investigation, he must carefully avoid.

In this connection consider the following:—

I very much regret that it should have been thought necessary to suggest to you that I am brought here to "hurry you against the law and beyond the evidence." I hope I have too much regard for justice, and too much respect for my own character, to attempt either; and were I to make such attempt, I am sure that in this court nothing can be carried against the law, and that gentlemen, intelligent and just as you are, are not, by any power, to be hurried beyond the evidence. Though I

[1] Redfield Proctor, United States Senate, March 17, 1898.

Persuasion in the Introduction

could well have wished to shun this occasion, I have not felt at liberty to withhold my professional assistance, when it is supposed that I may be in some degree useful in investigating and discovering the truth respecting this most extraordinary murder. It has seemed to be a duty incumbent on me, as on every other citizen, to do my best and my utmost to bring to light the perpetrators of this crime. Against the prisoner at the bar, as an individual, I cannot have the slightest prejudice. I would not do him the smallest injury or injustice. But I do not affect to be indifferent to the discovery and the punishment of this deep guilt. I cheerfully share in the opprobrium, how great so ever it may be, which is cast on those who feel and manifest an anxious concern that all who had a part in planning, or a hand in executing, this deed of midnight assassination, may be brought to answer for their enormous crime at the bar of public justice.[1]

Sincerity. Another quality of paramount importance to the arguer is sincerity. This he must really possess if he is to be eminently successful. To feign it is almost impossible; some word or expression, some gesture or inflection of the voice, the very attitude of the insincere arguer will betray his real feelings. It he tries to arouse an emotion that he himself does not feel, his affectation will be apparent and his effort a failure. There are few things that an audience resents more than being tricked into an expression of feeling. If they even

[1] The Works of Daniel Webster, Vol. VI, p. 51. Little, Brown & Co., Boston, 1857.

mistrust that a speaker is trying to deceive them, that he is arguing merely for personal gain or reputation and has no other interest in the case, no desire to establish the truth, they will not only withhold their confidence, but will also become prejudiced against him. It is usually inviting disaster to champion a cause in which one is not interested heart and soul. Of course in class room work the student cannot always avoid taking a false position, and the training he receives thereby is excellent, but he cannot make his persuasion of the highest type of effectiveness unless he honestly and sincerely believes what he says, and feels the emotions he would arouse.

An appeal to some emotion. One of the strongest forms of conciliation is the direct appeal to a dominant emotion. If an arguer can find some common ground on which to meet his audience, some emotion by which they may be moved, he can usually obtain a personal hold that will overcome hostility and lack of interest. In deciding what emotion to arouse, he must make as careful and thorough a study of his audience as he can. In general, the use of conviction need vary but little to produce the same results on different men; processes of pure reasoning are essentially the same

Persuasion in the Introduction

the world around. But with persuasion the case
is different; emotions are varied, and in each separate instance the arguer must carefully consider
the ruling passions and ideals of his audience. The
hopes and aspirations of a gang of ignorant miners
would differ widely from the desires of an assembly
of college students, or of a coterie of metropolitan
capitalists. Education, wealth, social standing, politics, religion, race, nationality, every motive that
is likely to have weight with the audience should be
taken into consideration. Remembering that he has
to choose between such diverse emotions as ambition, fear, hatred, love, patriotism, sense of duty,
honor, justice, self-interest, pleasure, and revenge,
the arguer must make his selection with the greatest
care, and then drive home the appeal with all the
force and eloquence at his command. The higher
and nobler the emotion he can arouse, the greater
and more permanent will be the result. If the
audience is such that he can successfully arouse no
higher feeling than that of self-interest or revenge,
he will, of necessity, have to appeal to these motives;
but whenever he can, he should appeal to the noblest
sentiments of mankind.

A famous illustration of the effectiveness of this
sort of conciliation is found in Wendell Phillips'

Persuasion in the Introduction

oration entitled *The Murder of Lovejoy*. By appealing to their reverence for the past, he silenced the mob that had come to break up the meeting, and in the end he won over the house that had been packed against him.

We have met for the freest discussion of these resolutions, and the events which gave rise to them. I hope I shall be permitted to express my surprise at the sentiments of the last speaker, surprise not only at such sentiments from such a man, but at the applause they have received within these walls. A comparison has been drawn between the events of the Revolution and the tragedy at Alton. We have heard it asserted here, in Faneuil Hall, that Great Britain had a right to tax the colonies, and we have heard the mob at Alton, the drunken murderers of Lovejoy, compared to those patriot fathers who threw the tea overboard! Fellow citizens, is this Faneuil Hall doctrine? . . . Sir, when I heard the gentleman lay down principles which place the murderers of Alton side by side with Otis and Hancock, with Quincy and Adams, I thought those pictured lips (pointing to the portraits in the Hall) would have broken into voice to rebuke the recreant American — the slanderer of the dead. The gentleman said that he should sink into insignificance if he dared to gainsay the principles of these resolutions. Sir, for the sentiments he has uttered, on soil consecrated by the prayers of Puritans and the blood of patriots, the earth should have yawned and swallowed him up.[1]

Specific directions for arousing the emotions are hard to give. The appeal must suit both the audi-

[1] American Orations, Vol. II, page 102. G. P. Putnam's Sons.

Persuasion in the Introduction

ence and the occasion, and until these are known, suggestions are not particularly helpful. When no better plan for conciliating an audience seems practicable, speakers and writers try to arouse *interest* in the discussion. There are several convenient methods for accomplishing this result.

1. **Importance of the subject.** One of the commonest methods of arousing interest in an audience apathetic and indifferent is to impress upon them the importance and gravity of the question at issue. Matters thought to be trival are apt to receive scant attention. This fact is so universally recognized that many writers and speakers attempt at the very outset to show that upon the correct solution of the problem at hand depend serious and far-reaching results. It is seldom enough merely to state that a subject is important; its seriousness should be made apparent. This method is very popular. Whenever one feels it necessary to open an argument with persuasion, but is at loss to know how to do so, he may well resort to this device. While it does not, perhaps, constitute the strongest possible appeal, yet it is eminently serviceable, since, if handled properly, it does arouse interest, and, moreover, it applies to many cases.

Persuasion in the Introduction

Several examples will show how this method is commonly used:—

Mr. President, the question now about to be discussed by this body is in my judgment the most important that has attracted the attention of Congress or the country since the formation of the Constitution. It affects every interest, great and small, from the slightest concern of the individual to the largest and most comprehensive interest of the nation.[1]

No city ever had such a problem in passenger transportation to solve, and no city of any pretensions has solved it much worse. London is not in the strict sense a town, but rather a "province of houses." The county of London, as everybody knows, is only a part of the Metropolis. The four millions and a half of residents enclosed by the legal ring-fence of the County are supplemented by two millions more who live in groups of suburbs included within the wide limits of "Greater London"; while even beyond that large tract of southeastern England, with its six millions and a half of inhabitants, are many towns and villages, populous and increasing, which are concerned with the question of Metropolitan locomotion.[2]

2. Timeliness of the subject. To show that a subject is timely is another effective device for arousing interest. As most people wish to keep pace with the times and face the issues of the day, it is natural and forceful to introduce an argument by showing that the subject is being discussed elsewhere, or by showing how an event or sequence of

---

[1] J. P. Jones, United States Senate, May 12, 1890.
[2] The Fortnightly Review, Jan. 1, 1902.

Persuasion in the Introduction

events places the problem before the public. The arguer calls attention to the fact that the question does not belong to the past or to the distant future, but is of immediate interest and must be settled at once.

As the day of the Cuban Convention for the framing and adoption of a constitution approaches, the question of Cuban independence assumes greater, and still greater, proportions, and the eyes of the American people are beginning to turn anxiously toward the Pearl of the Antilles. By the time this article appears in print, delegates to the convention will have been elected, and interest in the convention itself will have become widespread. The task I have set before me is briefly to review the situation, and to discuss the probable results to be expected from a number of causes, remote as well as proximate.[1]

The recent objection made in Germany that American prestige might suffer should there be diminution in our Berlin Embassy's social brilliancy has stirred Congress from apathy regarding American representatives abroad. Congressmen are coming to realize that brains, not money, ought to form the first passport to a candidate's favor, agreeable adjunct as the money may be.[2]

3. Appeal for one's self. The safest method of stirring the emotions is to make an appeal in behalf of the subject, but occasionally a writer or speaker who is truly sincere, who is contending against unfortunate circumstances, and is not seeking personal

[1] Charles Warren Currier. The Forum, October, 1900.
[2] The Outlook, April 18, 1908, p. 844.

aggrandizement, may arouse interest by making an appeal on his own behalf. He may present some personal reason why the audience should be interested and give him a respectful hearing; he calls attention not primarily to his subject, but to his connection with it, or to some circumstance in his own life. This method is hedged about with several pitfalls: it may expose one to the charge of egotism, of insincerity, or of false modesty; and it may draw the attention of the audience away from the matter in hand. To use this method successfully one should possess consummate tact and thorough knowledge of human nature.

The following opening of a speech by Abraham Lincoln at Columbus, Ohio, shows how he used this device to gain the sympathy of the audience:—

Fellow-citizens of the State of Ohio: I cannot fail to remember that I appear for the first time before an audience in this now great State,— an audience that is accustomed to hear such speakers as Corwin, and Chase, and Wade, and many other renowned men; and remembering this, I feel that it will be well for you, as for me, that you should not raise your expectations to that standard to which you would have been justified in raising them had one of these distinguished men appeared before you. You would perhaps be only preparing a disappointment for yourselves, and, as a consequence of your disappointment, mortification for me. I hope, therefore, that you will commence with very moderate expectations; and

Persuasion in the Introduction

perhaps, if you will give me your attention, I shall be able to interest you in a moderate degree.[1]

These, then, are the suggestions offered for conciliating an audience: Be modest; be fair; be sincere; and appeal to some strong emotion. To make this appeal successfully, study your audience. In case of inability to arouse any stronger feeling, appeal to the interest of the people by showing that the subject is important, or timely, or both; or show that you have some personal claim upon the audience.

These directions are far from complete. Anything like an exhaustive treatment of this subject would in itself constitute a book. The advice offered here, however, should be of considerable value to one who has difficulty in getting a written argument or a debate successfully launched. The student should supplement this chapter with careful study of the work of proficient writers. If he will notice how they have gained success in this particular, and if he will imitate them, he is bound to improve his own compositions. The principal dangers to be avoided consist of going to extremes. The conciliatory part of the introduction should not be so meager that it will fail to accomplish its

[1] Complete Works of Abraham Lincoln, Vol. I, p. 538. Nicolay & Hay. Century Company.

Persuasion in the Introduction

purpose, nor should it be so elaborate and artificial as to hamper the onward movement of the argument. The important thing is to gain the good will and the attention of the audience, and, other things being equal, the shorter the introduction the better. Further directions for the spoken argument may be found in the chapter entitled *Debate*.

EXERCISES

A. Criticise the following introductory passages for persuasiveness, pointing out specifically the methods of conciliation used, and any defects that may be found :—

1. The building of the Panama Canal is a topic of interest and importance to every American. Not only do we wish to see our country build the canal successfully, but we also desire to see built the best canal that the world has ever known. There is no doubt that the canal is necessary ; the great loss of time and money, the annual sacrifice of ships and lives involved in the passage around the " Horn," not to mention the expense and congestion of the railroad freight systems across the continent, plainly show the need of quicker ship communication between the two oceans.

2. I stand here to raise the last voice that ever can be heard this side the judgment seat of God in behalf of the personal honor and judicial integrity of this respondent. I fully realize the responsibilities of my position, and I shall endeavor to meet them as best I can. I also realize as deeply as any other man can how important it is not only to my client but to every American man, woman, and child that justice shall be done and true deliverance made.

3. The opening of the racing season in New York, at the Aqueduct track on Long Island, gives a fresh oppor-

Persuasion in the Introduction

tunity for observation of the conditions under which horse-racing, and more especially gambling on horse races, is carried on. The announcement of the racing managers that certain "reforms" had been inaugurated in the control of the gambling makes the opportunity of especial interest.

4. I approach the discussion of this bill and the kindred bills and amendments pending in the two Houses with unaffected diffidence. No problem is submitted to us of equal importance and difficulty. Our action will affect the value of all the property of all the people of the United States, and the wages of labor of every kind, and our trade and commerce with all the world. In the consideration of such a question we should not be controlled by previous opinions or bound by local interests, but with the light of experience and full knowledge of all the complicated facts involved, give to the subject the best judgment which imperfect human nature allows.

5. Each generation has the power to shape its own destinies; and had Washington and his fellow patriots been governed by warnings against a departure from traditions, our present form of government would never have been established, the Constitution would have been rejected by the States, and untold evils would have resulted. Madison, when arguing for the adoption of the Constitution, met arguments very like to those now being made in favor of political isolation.

6. As a race they have withered from the land. Their arrows are broken and their springs are dried up; their cabins are in the dust. Their council fire has long since gone out on the shore, and their war cry is fast dying out to the untrodden West. Slowly and sadly they climb the mountains and read their doom in the setting sun. They are shrinking before the mighty tide which is pressing them away; they must soon hear the roar of the last wave, which will settle over them forever. Ages hence

43

the inquisitive white man, as he stands by some growing city, will ponder on the structure of their disturbed remains and wonder to what manner of person they belonged. They will live only in the songs and chronicles of their exterminators. Let these be faithful to their rude virtues as men, and pay due tribute to their unhappy fate as a people.

7. (During the Civil War England largely favored the South. To counteract this feeling Henry Ward Beecher spoke in many of the principal cities in behalf of Northern interests. In Liverpool he met an audience that was extremely hostile. The following is the introduction to his speech.) For more than twenty-five years I have been made perfectly familiar with popular assemblies in all parts of my country except the extreme South. There has not been for the whole of that time a single day of my life when it would have been safe for me to go south of Mason and Dixon's line in my own country, and all for one reason: my solemn, earnest, persistent testimony against that which I consider to be the most atrocious thing under the sun — the system of American slavery in a great free republic. (Cheers.) I have passed through that early period when right of free speech was denied me. Again and again I have attempted to address audiences that, for no other crime than that of free speech, visited me with all manner of contumelious epithets; and now since I have been in England, although I have met with greater kindness and courtesy on the part of most than I deserved, yet, on the other hand, I perceive that the Southern influence prevails to some extent in England. (Applause and uproar.) It is my old acquaintance; I understand it perfectly—(laughter)—and I have always held it to be an unfailing truth that where a man had a cause that would bear examination he was perfectly willing to have it spoken about. (Applause.) And when in Manchester I saw those huge placards, " Who is Henry

Persuasion in the Introduction

Ward Beecher?" (laughter, cries of "Quite right," and applause), and when in Liverpool I was told that there were those blood-red placards, purporting to say what Henry Ward Beecher has said, and calling upon Englishmen to suppress free speech, I tell you what I thought. I thought simply this, "I am glad of it." (Laughter.) Why? Because if they had felt perfectly secure, that *you* are the minions of the South and the slaves of slavery, they would have been perfectly still. (Applause and uproar.) And, therefore, when I saw so much nervous apprehension that, if I were permitted to speak — (hisses and applause) — when I found they were afraid to have me speak — (hisses, laughter, and "No, no!") — when I found that they considered my speaking damaging to their cause — (applause) — when I found that they appealed from facts and reasonings to mob law — (applause and uproar) — I said, no man need tell me what the heart and secret counsel of these men are. They tremble and are afraid. (Applause, laughter, hisses, "No, no!" and a voice, "New York mob.") Now, personally, it is of very little consequence to me whether I speak here to-night or not. (Laughter and cheers.) But one thing is very certain, if you do permit me to speak here to-night, you will hear very plain talking. (Applause and hisses.) You will not find a man — (interruption) — you will not find me to be a man that dared to speak about Great Britain three thousand miles off, and then is afraid to speak to Great Britain when he stands on her shores. (Immense applause and hisses.) And if I do not mistake the tone and temper of Englishmen, they had rather have a man who opposes them in a manly way — (applause from all parts of the hall) — than a sneak that agrees with them in an unmanly way. (Applause and "Bravo!") Now, if I can carry you with me by sound convictions, I shall be immensely glad (applause); but if I cannot carry you with me by facts and sound arguments, I do not wish

45

Persuasion in the Introduction

you to go with me at all; and all that I ask is simply FAIR PLAY. (Applause, and a voice, " You shall have it, too.")

Those of you who are kind enough to wish to favor my speaking,— and you will observe that my voice is slightly husky from having spoken almost every night in succession for some time past,— those who wish to hear me will do me the kindness simply to sit still; and I and my friends the Secessionists will make all the noise. (Laughter.)

B. On the affirmative side of the following propositions, write conciliatory introductions, of about two hundred words each, suited to the audiences indicated :—

AN AUDIENCE OF COLLEGE STUDENTS.

1. All colleges should abolish hazing.
2. Fraternities tend to destroy college spirit.
3. A classical education is not worth while.
4. All colleges should abolish secret class societies.
5. Intercollegiate athletic contests are harmful to a college.

AN AUDIENCE OF WORKINGMEN.

6. Strikes are barren of profitable results.
7. Unions are detrimental to the laboring man.
8. The concentration of great wealth in the hands of a few men benefits industrial conditions.

CHAPTER IV

THE INTRODUCTION — CONVICTION

As soon as the persuasive portion of an introduction has rendered the audience friendly, attentive, and open to conviction, the process of reasoning should begin. First of all, it is the duty of the arguer to see that the meaning of the proposition is perfectly clear both to himself and to all the people whom he wishes to reach. If the arguer does not thoroughly comprehend his subject, he is likely to produce only a jumble of facts and reasoning, or at best he may establish a totally different proposition from the one that confronts him; if the audience fails to understand just what is being proved, they remain uninfluenced. The amount of explanation required to show what the proposition means varies according to the intelligence of the people addressed and their familiarity with the subject. ·

DEFINITION.

To begin with, if there are any unfamiliar words in the proposition, any terms or expressions that

Conviction in the Introduction

are liable to be misunderstood or not comprehended
instantly, they must be defined. At this point the
arguer has to exercise considerable judgment both
in determining what words to define and in choosing
a definition that is accurate and clear. Synonyms
are almost always untrustworthy or as incomprehensible as the original word, and other dictionary
definitions are usually framed either in too technical
language to be easily grasped or in too general language to apply inevitably to the case at hand.

Definition by authority. As a rule, the very
best definitions that can be used are *quotations* from
the works of men distinguished for their knowledge
in the special subject to which the word to be defined belongs. The eminent economist defines economic terms; the statesman, political terms; the jur-
ist, legal terms; the scientist, scientific terms; the
theologian, the meaning of religious phraseology.
To present these definitions accurately, and to be
sure of the author's meaning, one should take the
quotations directly from the author's work itself. If,
however, this source is not at hand, or if time for
research is lacking, one may often find in legal and
economic dictionaries and in encyclopædias the very
quotations that he wishes to use in defining a term.
It is always well, in quoting a definition, to tell

Conviction in the Introduction

who the authority is, and in what book, in what volume, and on what page the passage occurs.

Another convenient way of using definition by authority is not to quote the entire definition but to *summarize* it. Frequently an authoritative definition is so exhaustive that it covers several pages or even chapters of a book. In such a case the arguer may well condense the definition into his own words, not omitting, however, to name the sources used. The following example is an excellent illustration of this method:—

> The bearing of the Monroe Doctrine on all these contentions and counter contentions is not at once evident to the casual observer. . . . Of course with changing times its meaning has changed also, for no one attempts to declare it to be as immutable as the law of the Medes and Persians. It is applied in various ways to meet varying conditions. Nevertheless, I may say I believe, after a perusal of the more important works on the subject, that during the forescore years of its existence two principles have steadily underlain it: (1) that Europe shall acquire no more territory for permanent occupation upon this continent; (2) that Europe shall affect the destinies of, that is exert influence over, no American state.*

> * A. B. Hart, *Foundations of American Foreign Policy,* chap. VII; J. W. Foster, *A Century of American Diplomacy,* chap. XII; J. A. Kasson, *The Evolution of the Constitution of the United States of America,* pages 221ff.[1]

Definition by illustration. Since the purpose of

[1] Nutter, Hersey & Greenough, Specimens of Prose Composition, p. 218.

each step in the reasoning portion of the introduction is to convey information accurately, quickly, and, above all else, clearly, a particularly good method for defining terms is by illustration. In using this method, one holds up to view a concrete example of the special significance of the word that is being explained. He shows how the law, or custom, or principle, or whatever is being expounded works in actual practice. For example, if he is advocating the superiority of the large college over the small college, he should define each term by giving specific examples of large colleges and of small colleges. The advantage of this method lies in its simplicity and clearness, qualities which enable the audience to understand the discussion without much conscious effort on their part. Investigation reveals that the definitions of great writers and speakers are replete with illustration. Whenever the student of argumentation has something to define that is particularly intricate or hard to understand, he should illustrate it. If he fails to find already prepared an illustrative definition that exactly fits his needs, he will often do well to learn just what the term means, and then make his own illustration.

Consider how this method has been used. The

Conviction in the Introduction

Hon. Charles Emory Smith defines reciprocity as follows :—

Its principle, rightly understood, is axiomatic. Brazil grows coffee and makes no machinery. We make machinery and grow no coffee. She needs the fabrics of our forges and factories, and we need the fruit of her tropical soil. We agree to concessions for her coffee and she agrees to concessions for our machinery. That is reciprocity.

The following is a definition of free silver by The Hon. Edward O. Leech, former Director of the Mint :—

It is important to understand clearly and exactly what the free coinage of silver under present conditions means. It may be defined as the right of anyone to deposit silver of any kind at a mint of the United States, and have every 371¼ grains of pure silver (now worth in its uncoined state about 52 cents) stamped, free of charge, "One Dollar," which dollar shall be a full legal tender at its face value in the payment of debts and obligations of all kinds, public and private, in the United States.

In upholding his opinion that a majority of the members of the House of Representatives have the right to make the rules governing parliamentary procedure in the House, The Hon. Thomas B. Reed carefully defines the term " rights ":—

Conviction in the Introduction

It is the fault of most discussions which are decided incorrectly that they are decided by the misuse of terms. Unfortunately, words have very little precision, and mean one thing to one man and a different thing to another. Words are also used with one meaning and quoted with another. When men speak of the rights of minorities and claim for them the sacredness of established law, they are correct or incorrect according as they interpret the word "rights."

A man has a right to an estate in fee simple, a right to land, and there is no right more indisputable under our system. Nothing but the supreme law can take the estate away, and then only after compensation. The same man has a right of passage over land used as a highway, but his town or county can take that privilege away from him without his consent and without compensation. In both cases the man has rights, but the rights are entirely different, and the difference arises from the nature of things. It is good for the community, or at least it has been so thought, that a man should have unrestricted right over his land. On it he can build as high as heaven or dig as deep as a probable hereafter. This is not because it is pleasant for the man, but because it is best for the community. Therefore his right to build or dig is limited by the right of eminent domain — the right of the whole people to take his property at any time for the common benefit on paying its value.

For the same reason the right of a man to walk over the land of a roadway is an inferior right which may more easily be taken from him; for if it be more convenient for the whole community that nobody should walk over that land, each man's right, which is a perfect right while it exists, is taken away from him, and he alone bears the loss.

It is hardly necessary to multiply examples in order to lay a foundation for the assertion that the rights, so

52

called, of any man or set of men, have their foundation
only in the common good.

EXPLANATION.

Not only must the arguer define the unfamiliar
words that occur in the proposition, but he must
also explain the meaning of the proposition *taken
as a whole*. Since an audience often has neither
the inclination nor the opportunity to give a proposition careful thought and study, the disputant
himself must make clear the matter in dispute, and
show exactly where the difference in opinion between the affirmative and the negative lies. This
process is of great importance; it removes the
subject of dispute from the realm of mere words —
words which arranged in a formal statement are
to many often incomprehensible — and brings out
clearly the *idea* that is to be supported or condemned.

To discover just what the proposition means, the
arguer must weigh each word, carefully noting its
meaning and its significance in the proposition.
To neglect a single word is disastrous. An intercollegiate debate was once lost because the affirmative side did not take into consideration the words
" present tendency " in the proposition, " *Resolved,*

Conviction in the Introduction

That the present tendency of labor unions is detrimental to the prosperity of the United States."
The negative side admitted everything that the affirmative established, namely, that unions are detrimental; and won by showing that their *tendcency* is beneficial. In another college debate on the subject, "*Resolved,* That the United States should immediately dispose of the Philippines," one side failed to meet the real point at issue because it ignored the word " immediately." A thorough explanation of the proposition would have shown the limitations that this word imposed upon the discussion.

In the next place, the arguer should usually present to the audience a brief history of the matter in dispute. Many debatable subjects are of such a nature that the arguer himself cannot, until he has studied the history of the proposition, fully understand what constitutes the clash in opinion between the affirmative and the negative sides. To understand the debate, the audience must possess this same information. A history of the idea contained in the proposition would be absolutely necessary to render intelligible such subjects as: " The aggressions of England in the Transvaal are justifiable "; " The United States should re-establish reciprocity with Canada "; " Football reform is advisable."

In the last place, the arguer must give his audience all essential information concerning the matter in dispute. For example, if the proposition is, " Naturalization laws in the United States should be more stringent," a mere definition of " naturalization laws " is not enough; the disputant must tell just what naturalization laws exist at the present time, and just how stringent they are to-day. Again, if the subject is, " The United States army should be enlarged," the arguer must tell exactly how large the army is now. If the proposition is, " The right of suffrage should be further limited by an educational test," the arguer must state what limits now exist, and he must also tell what is meant by " an educational test." In a debate the work of the affirmative and of the negative differ slightly at this point. Since the proposition reads *an educational test,* the advocate for the affirmative has the privilege of upholding any sort of educational test that he wishes to defend, provided only that it comes within the limits of " an educational test." He may say that the test should consist of a knowledge of the alphabet, or he may advocate an examination in higher mathematics; *but he is under obligation to outline carefully and thoroughly some specific system.* The negative, on the other hand, must be prepared to overthrow whatever system is brought forward. If the affirmative fails to outline any system, the negative has only to call attention to this fact to put the affirmative in a very embarrassing position.

The following quotations are good illustrations of how a proposition may be explained:—

The supremely significant and instructive fact, in the dealings of society with crime in our day, and one which has not been fully grasped as yet by the legal profession, not even by those who practice in criminal courts, and who should be familiar with it, is this: We have now two classes of institutions fundamentally distinct in character and purpose, both of which are designed by society, erected and conducted at public expense, for the purpose of dealing with criminals. The most numerous class of these institutions consists of prisons, in which to confine men for terms specified by the trial courts as penalties for their offenses. The laws, under which offenders are sentenced to these prisons, aim at classifying crimes according to the degree of guilt they imply, and assigning to each of them the penalty which it deserves. Thus, to these prisons are sent men sentenced to confinement for two, five, ten, fourteen, or thirty years, or for life, according to the name which the law attaches to the crime proved upon them; and each man, when he has served the prescribed term, is turned loose upon society. The other class of institutions includes what are known as "reformatories." The fundamental principle here is

Conviction in the Introduction

that an offender is sent to them not for a term, but for a specified work. It is assumed that his character and habits unfit him for social life. For reasons to be found in his own nature, he cannot yet be trusted with freedom and the responsibilities of citizenship. But he may possess the capacity to become an honest, industrious, and useful citizen. To the reformatory, then, he is sent to be educated; to be trained to habits of industry; above all, to be disciplined in the habit of looking forward to the future with the consciousness that his welfare and happiness to-morrow depend on his conduct to-day, and that he is constantly shaping his own destiny. He is expected to remain until it satisfactorily appears that this training is effective, and he may then go forth with a prospect of leading an honest and respectable life. This, in brief, is the distinction between these two classes of institutions.

For a generation past, these two kinds of prisons have been standing side by side in New York, Massachusetts, and other States. Each of them has received many thousands of criminals under sentence for grave offenses. Each of them has sent out thousands of inmates into the world of human society, with whatever impress the life, teachings, and associations of the institutions could make upon their natures, as a preparation for their after career. What is the result? [1]

Congress has at last decided that the long-talked-of canal shall be built, and shall be built at Panama. Those issues no longer confront us. The question now to be decided concerns the kind of canal that shall be constructed. Two plans have been suggested: the lock-canal plan and the sea-level plan. The advocates of the lock-canal plan aim to build a gigantic dam in the valley of the Chagres River; the enormous artificial lake thus formed being used as part of the passageway for the

[1] Charlton T. Lewis, in North American Review, August, 1904.

vessels. They say that this lake will be at an elevation of about eighty-five feet above mean sea-level; the passage to and from it will be made by means of canals at both ends, each canal containing three locks. Thus there will be, if this plan is adopted, six locks in the entire system. The canal will be of sufficient width and depth to accommodate vessels of such size as may be expected to be built when the canal is completed.

If the canal is built at sea-level, it will be of the same depth and width as the lock-canal, but it will be at the level of the sea throughout its entire length. Owing to the fact that the Atlantic and the Pacific have a difference in extreme level of twenty feet, an automatic tide-lock will have to be installed. A small lake will also be built, merely to divert the Chagres and to furnish light and power.

The question that now confronts us is, "Which plan should be adopted?"

ISSUES.

Following the discovery of the real meaning of the proposition, comes the finding of the issues. Whenever a man in business, professional, or political life, or in any circumstances whatsoever, must determine upon some policy or come to some decision regarding theoretical or practical matters, he formulates his belief and chooses his line of action in accordance with the answers that he makes to certain questions either consciously or unconsciously present in his mind. For instance, if he considers the purchase of a certain piece of real

Conviction in the Introduction

estate, he says to himself: "Is the price fair?"
"Have I the money to invest?" "Can I sell or
use the property to good advantage?" "How much
pleasure shall I derive from it?" If he answers
these questions in one way, the purchase is likely
to be made; if in another, it is not. Again, a
board of college trustees may be considering the
abolishment of football. In arriving at a decision,
they are confronted with these questions: "Is the
game beneficial or detrimental to the player?"
"How does it affect the college as a whole?"
Those who favor the game will, of course, say that
it is a benefit to the player and the whole college;
while those who oppose it will maintain that it is a
detriment to all concerned. But evidently the same
questions must be met and answered by both sides.
These questions are called *issues*.

Issues are subdivisions of the subject under discussion, and are always essentially the same for any
given idea. The first requirement for the issues
of any proposition is that they be comprehensive;
that is, the sum of their ideas must equal the main
idea expressed in the proposition. To those who
are carrying on the discussion and to the audience,
if there be one, it must be perfectly evident that
these questions cover the entire field of controversy;

that if these questions are satisfactorily answered in one way or the other, the discussion is settled and nothing remains to be said. The second requirement is that the issues consider only disputed matter. A question that gives rise to no disagreement, that admittedly has but one answer, is never an issue. *Issues, therefore, may be defined as the questions that must be answered by both the affirmative and the negative sides of the proposition under discussion and that, if answered in one way, establish the proposition, and if answered in another way, overthrow it.*

The issues of a proposition exist independently of the side that is being upheld. The affirmative will find the same issues as the negative, but it rarely happens that two men will divide a proposition in exactly the same manner and thus state the issues in precisely the same language. If, however, the work of both has been fair and complete, their issues will not vary in any important particular. For example, under the subject, "The Federal government should own and operate the railroads of the United States," one person might give as issues :—

1. Has the government the right to take the roads without the consent of the present owners?

Conviction in the Introduction

2. Is the government financially able to buy the roads?

3. Does the present system contain serious defects?

4. Will the proposed system remove these defects without bringing in new evils equally serious?

Another might state as issues:—

1. Is the proposed plan practicable?

2. Will it benefit the people?

The issues in both instances, however, are essentially the same, as questions one and two of the first list are equivalent to one of the second; and three and four of the first, to two of the second.

At this point it may be well to mention a common error that must be guarded against. It often happens that a question is stated as an issue which is not a subdivision of the proposition at all, but is the entire proposition itself, framed in slightly different language. Such would be the error if the question, " Would the change be desirable? " were used as an issue for the proposition, " All state colleges should abolish military drill."

It sometimes happens that one is forced to defend or attack what has been called a " combined proposition, a proposition that contains two distinct subjects for argument. Such subjects are to be

Conviction in the Introduction

avoided as much as possible, but when they must be met, it is usually necessary to have two separate sets of issues. An example of such a proposition would be, " All American colleges and universities should adopt the honor system."

The only practicable method of finding the issues of a proposition is to question it from all pertinent points of view, and then to eliminate all questions that have no vital bearing on the subject, or that are acknowledged to have but one answer. The questions that remain are the issues. In using this method of analysis, one must be careful to consider the proposition in all its phases and details, and from both the affirmative and the negative sides. Neglect to give the subject thorough consideration often results in one's being suddenly confronted with an issue that he has not previously discovered and consequently cannot meet. Failure to cast aside all questions that are not real issues may cause equal embarrassment: an arguer never wishes to waste time and effort in establishing proof that is not essential to the argument, or that is admitted by the other side.

It is hardly possible even to suggest all the various kinds of questions that may be asked about debatable subjects. An arguer must depend largely

Conviction in the Introduction

upon his own judgment and common sense in analyzing each proposition that he meets. He may, however, find the issues of many propositions by carefully questioning them from certain important and comprehensive points of view. The list of standpoints indicated here is not exhaustive; only the more important and general standpoints are considered. The student should bear in mind that the following instructions are designed to teach him a practical method of analysis; they do not constitute a formula that can be applied in all instances.

First, the analysis of propositions of policy will be taken up; secondly, the analysis of propositions of fact.

PROPOSITIONS OF POLICY.

1. **Is the plan practicable?** Whenever a plan is proposed, first ask whether or not it is practicable. If those who oppose the idea can maintain that great obstacles exist which will prevent the undertaking of the project or hinder its execution, then the question of practicability constitutes an important issue. For instance, one who contemplates a thorough argument on the proposition, " The United States navy should be greatly enlarged," must prove

that the plan is, or is not, practicable. Plainly, such hindrances as enormous expense, inadequate facilities for building and repairing battleships, and the increased demand for officers and sailors render questionable the expediency of such a measure. This issue, however, is not found in connection with all propositions; it does not concern propositions that merely approve or condemn existing conditions or assert the occurrence of an event. For example, practicability does not enter into such subjects as these: "Strikes are justifiable"; "The present powers of the Speaker of the House of Representatives are dangerously great"; "Athletics have been excessively developed in American colleges and universities." But all propositions that advocate a change, that propose some new system of operation, usually have this issue involved. Such subjects are: "American cities should own and operate public plants for the furnishing of light, heat, and power"; "Military drill should be taught in the public schools"; "Porto Rico should be given a territorial form of government."

2. **Will the proposed plan be a moral benefit or detriment to those concerned?** Not all propositions, by any means, but many, are of such a character that they must be considered from the

Conviction in the Introduction

standpoint of morality. The arguer must ask whether the idea involved in the subject is morally right or wrong; whether it is morally beneficial or harmful. This point of view includes more than at first appears. It takes into consideration justice, duty, honesty, faithfulness, religion, everything that pertains to what is right or wrong. Under the proposition, "The treatment of the American Indians by the United States should be condemned," appears the moral issue, "What is our *duty* toward the people of this race?" The proposition, "Public libraries, museums, and art galleries should be open on Sunday," presents this issue, "Is the method of recreation afforded by the opening of these buildings in accordance with the teachings of the Christian religion?" The proposition, "Football is an undesirable college game," must be settled in part by the answer to the question, "Is the game beneficial or harmful to the player's character?"

3. Will the proposed plan be a material benefit or detriment? In the third place the proposition should be questioned from a material point of view, to determine whether the plan is, or is likely to be, a benefit or a detriment. In some form this issue will doubtless be found in connection with al-

5   65

Conviction in the Introduction

most every proposition of policy. In all systems of government, of business, and even of education, material betterment is invariably one of the ultimate objects sought. The question of national expansion presents the issue, " Will such a course add to the glory, the prestige, or the wealth of the nation ? " When a boy considers going to college, he desires to know whether a college education is a valuable asset in business, social, or professional life. An issue which puts to the touch the matter of personal gain is sure to involve a substantial portion of the controversy. The arguer who can decisively settle the question of dollars and cents always has a strong argument. Usually the issue involving the question of material benefit or detriment is plain and direct; sometimes, however, it is partially concealed. A man debating on the affirmative side of the proposition, " *Resolved,* That United States Senators should be elected by a direct popular vote of the people," may urge as a reason that such a method will result in purer politics. This particular line of argument he may carry no farther, taking it for granted that everyone will recognize the connection between honest office holders and material gain.

4. Will the proposed plan be an intellectual benefit or detriment? All propositions that deal with education or with other matters that pertain to man's progress and advancement should be viewed from an intellectual standpoint. No person in discussing a measure bearing upon the welfare of an individual, of a community, or of a nation, can afford to neglect questioning its influence for mental advancement or retrogression. Propositions relating to schools, colleges, and similar institutions, and propositions dealing with social and industrial conditions present this issue. Modern theories of government, both municipal and national, are frequently based to some extent upon the idea of teaching the people how to live and how to govern themselves. The policy of the United States in the Philippines and in the West Indies has been greatly influenced by the query, " How will it affect the intellectual welfare of the people concerned? "

5. **Will the proposed plan be a physical benefit or detriment?** All subjects that concern the life, health, strength, or in any way bear upon the physical well-being of man present this issue. An argument on government ownership of railroads would have to answer the question, " Under which system will fewer accidents occur? " All such propositions as, " Eight hours ought legally to constitute a working day "; " State boards of health

should compel all persons afflicted with contagious diseases to be quarantined "; " Football is an undesirable college game," give rise to the issue of physical welfare.

6. Will the proposed plan be a political benefit or detriment? If a plan is of such far-reaching significance that its adoption or rejection would affect a whole town, state, or nation, then its merits usually depend to some extent upon its political significance. The issue may take some such form as, " How will the system affect the country politically? " " Will the system encourage bribery and graft, or will it tend to do away with these evils? " " What will be its effect upon bossism? "

7. How has the plan succeeded where it has been tried? This question frequently occurs as an issue in connection with all sorts of propositions. Its importance and significance are so evident that no explanation is needed. The value of precedent is known to every one.

8. Does the present system contain serious evils? The asking of this question is frequently one of the very best ways to get at the heart of a proposition of policy. To be sure, this question overlaps and embraces several other questions that have been suggested, but a comprehensive issue like this is sometimes preferable from the standpoint both of the arguer and of the audience. It removes from the arguer the necessity of classifying each evil under the head of *moral, financial, intellectual,* etc.; and in many cases it results in an argument more easily understood by the audience. In some form this issue applies to nearly all political, economic, and financial propositions.

9. If the present system does contain serious evils, will the proposed system remove them? Equal in importance with the question as to whether the existing system is defective, is the question as to whether the proposed system will remove these defects, without, of course, introducing equally great disadvantages. These two issues almost invariably go together; they set the system advocated by the affirmative and the system advocated by the negative side by side, and compare and contrast each with the other.

10. If the present system contains serious evils, is the proposed system the only remedy? This last question is very closely connected with the two preceding questions. The whole discussion may hinge not on whether evils exist, but on how they shall be remedied. If the argument takes this turn, the advocates of a certain system must show that their plan is the only one suitable for adoption, or, at least, is the best plan, while the negative must introduce and uphold a totally different scheme. For instance, under the proposition, "The United States army should be greatly enlarged," the first two issues would probably be these: "Is the present army adequate to protect the nation?" and "Is the enlargement of the army the *only* means of rendering the nation safe from invasion?"

PROPOSITIONS OF FACT.

1. Does the proposition state a possible truth? To find the issues of a proposition of fact, first ask whether the occurrence in question could have happened or the condition alleged in the proposition could possibly have existed. This question is so important that if it can conclusively be answered in the negative the discussion is ended. Legal proceedings invariably center around some form of a proposition of fact. In the criminal court a man to prove his innocence has only to establish an alibi or prove physical inability to commit the crime with which he is charged. Not always, of course, does the question of possibility constitute an issue, since frequently the possibility is admitted. Such would be the case if the following propositions came up for discussion: " Joan of Arc was burned at the stake "; " Nero was guilty of burning Rome." In these instances possibility gives way to probability.

2. **Does the proposition state a probable truth?** If the question of possibility has been answered affirmatively or inconclusively, the issue of probability next arises. In connection with many propositions of fact this is the most important issue to be encountered. Unless a condition or an event — its possibility being admitted — can be affirmed or denied by reliable witnesses who testify from their own personal knowledge of the matter, the most that any arguer can do is to establish a balance of probability. Those who believe that Bacon wrote the plays attributed to Shakespeare try to show how improbable it is that a man like Shakespeare could have produced such works, and how very likely it is that Bacon was the real author. Many criminals are convicted or acquitted on evidence that establishes merely a strong probability of guilt or of innocence.

71

Conviction in the Introduction

3. Is there any direct evidence bearing on the proposition? In the third place, a person who is trying to prove or disprove a proposition of fact must consider the direct evidence involved. Indirect evidence tends to establish the possibility or probability that a statement is true or false, while direct evidence asserts that it *is* true or false. Direct evidence on the question, " Country roads in New England are inferior to those of the Middle West," would not be a description of the topographical and geographical features of both regions, for this information could at its best establish only a strong probability; direct evidence on this subject would be the testimony of people who have investigated the roads, and could thus speak from direct personal knowledge.

This issue of direct evidence has two phases. The arguer must ask, " Is any direct evidence available? " and " If there is any, what is its value? " It is easily seen that not all evidence is equally reliable. Both the man and what he says must be tested: the man for such qualities as truthfulness, intelligence, and experience; the statements for consistency and general credibility. The tests of evidence are given in detail in another chapter.

Conviction in the Introduction

TESTS FOR ISSUES.

After an arguer has secured his list of issues, he should test his work by asking the four following questions :—

1. Does each issue really bear upon the proposition?

2. Is each issue a subdivision of the proposition, or is it the proposition itself formulated in different language?

3. Does each issue comprise only disputed matter?

4. Do the issues, taken collectively, consider all phases of the proposition?

Several illustrations will show more plainly just what issues are and how they are used in connection with other parts of an introduction.

Shall Greek be Taught in High Schools?

In taking up the discussion of Greek in the high schools, I shall consider these three questions: First, is Greek more valuable than other studies in training the mind? Second, does the study of Greek acquaint us with the best that has been known and said in the world, and, therefore, with the history of the human spirit? And third, where shall Greek be taught? [1]

[1] W. F. Webster, The Forum, December, 1899, page 459.

Conviction in the Introduction

Does Colonization Pay?

The points to be considered in determining the somewhat mercenary question, "Does Colonization Pay?" as viewed with regard to the interests of the colonizing country, are: (1) the market that the colonies afford for the goods which the colonizing country has to sell; and whether control gives to the mother-country a larger share of their market than she would have without that control; (2) the supplies the colonies are able to furnish for use in the mother-country; and whether the purchase of these supplies from the colonies proves more advantageous to the mother-country than if they should be purchased from other parts of the world; (3) the advantages, if any, which accrue to the native population of the country controlled.[1]

The following passage, taken from Daniel Webster's speech in which, as counsel for the city of Boston, he argues that a certain piece of land has not become a public highway, is a good illustration of an introduction on what was virtually a proposition of fact. Notice with what skill he cast aside all irrelevant matter and reduced the proposition to clearly stated and indisputable issues:—

If this street, or land, or whatever it may be, has become and now is a public highway, it must have become so in one of three ways, and to these points I particularly call your honors' attention.

1st. It must have either become a highway by having

[1] O. P. Austin, The Forum, January, 1900, p. 623.

been regularly laid out according to usage and law; or

2nd. By *dedication* as such by those having the power to dedicate it, and acceptance and adoption so far as they are required; or

3d. As a highway by long user, without the existence of proof of any original laying out, or dedication.

It is not pretended by any one that the land in question is a highway, upon the last of these grounds. I shall therefore confine myself to the consideration of the other two questions; namely, Was there ever a formal and regular laying out of a street here? or was there ever a regular and sufficient dedication and acceptance?[1]

PARTITION.

In college debate, though not frequently elsewhere, the issues as a rule are immediately followed by a series of statements that show how each issue is to be answered. These statements constitute what is known as the *partition*. When a partition is made, each statement becomes a main point to be established by proof in the discussion. The following portion of a student's argument contains both the issues and the partition:—

In considering, then, whether colleges should adopt the system of exempting from final examinations all students who have attained an average daily grade of eighty-five per cent. or over, we have only to consider the effect such a rule would have upon the students, individually

[1] The Works of Daniel Webster, Vol. VI, p. 186. Little, Brown & Co., Boston, 1857.

Conviction in the Introduction

and collectively. Would the system raise or lower the standard of scholarship? Would it assist or retard the growth of other qualities which a college course should develop? The negative will oppose the adoption of this rule by establishing the three following points:—

1. Such a system will lower the scholarship both of those who are exempted from examinations and of those who are not.

2. Such a system will foster dishonesty, jealousy, and conceit.

3. Such a system will deprive those who are exempted from examinations of valuable discipline in preparing for examinations and in taking the examinations.

There are several forms in which the partition may be expressed: it may consist of a single sentence that indicates how the issues are to be answered; it may consist of the issues themselves turned into declarative sentences so that they read in favor of the side being upheld; or it may answer each issue by means of several statements. The following will illustrate the several methods:—

Proposition: *Resolved,* That football is an undesirable college game.

Issues: 1. Does football benefit or injure the player?

2. Does football benefit or injure the college as a whole?

Conviction in the Introduction

Partition (negative):

First method.

1. We will establish our side of the argument by proving that in each case football is a benefit.

Second method.

1. Football benefits the player.
2. Football benefits the college as a whole.

Third method.

1. Football benefits the player physically.
2. Football benefits the player mentally.
3. Football benefits the player morally.
4. Football benefits the students who do not participate in the game.
5. Intercollegiate football games advertise the college.

The partition is usually found in college debate because in a contest of this sort absolute clearness is a prerequisite for success. As but little interest customarily centers around the subject itself, each debater knows that if he is to make any impression on the audience he must so arrange his argument that it will, with a minimum amount of effort on the part of the listener, be clear to every one. To one reading an argument, a partition, unless of the simplest kind, will probably seem superfluous; to one listening to a speech in which he is truly interested, the partition may seem labored. But when the whole interest centers in the method of presentation, and in the processes of reasoning rather than in the subject matter, the partition does increase the clearness of the argument, and should, therefore, be used.

By way of summary, then, it may be said that the work of conviction in the introduction is to show the relation between the proposition and the proof. The arguer accomplishes this task, first, by defining all words the meaning of which is not generally comprehended; secondly, by explaining, in the light of these definitions, the meaning of the proposition taken as a whole; thirdly, by discovering the issues through a careful process of analysis; and fourthly, by making a partition when he is engaged in debate and has reason to think that the audience will not see the connection between the issues and the discussion.

HOW TO INVESTIGATE A SUBJECT.

A student will hardly have reached this point in the study of Argumentation before finding it neces-

Conviction in the Introduction

sary to search for information that will assist him in the construction of his argument. To one unfamiliar with a library, a search after facts bearing upon a given subject is likely to prove tedious. For this reason a few words of advice concerning the proper way in which to use a library may be of great help to a beginner. Nothing, however, can be given here that will even approximate the value of a few hours' instruction by the librarian of the college in which the student is enrolled. In the absence of such instruction, one can seldom do better at the outset than to become familiar with indexes to periodical and contemporary literature, encyclopædias, government reports, and the library catalogue.

The best indexes are the *Reader's Guide, Poole's Index, The Annual Library Index,* and the *Current Events Index.* These give references to all articles published in the principal magazines and newspapers for many years. In these articles one will find almost limitless material on nearly every popular topic of the day — political, economic, scientific, social, educational. The writers, too, are often of national and even of international reputation, and the opinions and ideas given here are frequently as weighty and progressive as can be found. In searching through an index for articles upon a certain subject, one should invariably look under several headings. For example, if one is seeking material in regard to the abolishment of baseball from the list of college sports, he ought not to consult just the one heading *baseball;* he should in addition look under *athletics, college sports,* and similar topics.

Other valuable sources of information are encyclopædias. They often give broad surveys and comprehensive digests that cannot readily be found elsewhere. Although they do not, as a rule, discuss subjects that are of mere local or present-day interest, yet the thorough searcher after evidence will usually do well to consult at least several. A fact worth bearing in mind is that in connection with these articles in encyclopædias, references are often given to books and articles that treat the subject very thoroughly.

In the next place, official publications frequently furnish invaluable help in regard to public problems. Both state governments and the national government constantly publish reports containing statistics, the opinions of experts, and suggestions for economic and political changes. Some of the most valuable of these documents for the purposes of the arguer are Census, Immigration, Education, and Interstate Commerce Commission reports, the messages of the

Conviction in the Introduction

Presidents, and the *Congressional Record*. There are indexes to all these, and one can easily find out how to use them.

Furthermore, one should not fail to consult the library catalogue. To be sure, if the books are catalogued only according to titles and authors, one will probably get little assistance from this source unless he knows beforehand what particular books or authors to search for. If, on the other hand, the books are also catalogued according to the subjects of which they treat, one can see almost at a glance what books the library has that bear upon the matter under investigation.

EXERCISES

A. Define the following terms:— monopoly, free trade, railway pooling, income tax, honorary degree, tutorial system of instruction, industrial education, classical education, German university method of study, vivisection, temperance, Indian agency system, yellow peril, graft, sensational, mass play, monarch, civilization, autonomy.

B. Criticise the issues that are given for the following propositions:—

1. *Resolved,* That in the United States naturalization laws should be more stringent.
   a. Are the present laws satisfactory?
   b. Have the results of the laws been satisfactory?
   c. Would a change be wise?

2 *Resolved,* That in the United States the reformatory system of imprisonment should be substituted for the punitive.

6

Conviction in the Introduction

    a. Is the reformatory system practicable?

    b. Does it reform the criminal?

    c. What has been its success thus far?

    d. Is it in accordance with modern civilization?

3. *Resolved,* That education in the United States should be compulsory to the age of sixteen.

    a. Is compulsory education practicable?

    b. Will compulsory education benefit the child?

    c. Will compulsory education benefit the public?

4. *Resolved,* That American universities should admit women on equal terms with men.

    a. Is woman's education as important as man's?

    b. Is coeducation a benefit to both sexes?

    c. Is coeducation a benefit to the college?

    d. Is the desirable system of separate education worth the extra money it costs?

5. *Resolved,* That in the United States there should be an educational test for voting.

    a. Is voting a privilege or a natural right?

    b. Ought illiterates to be excluded from the polls?

    c. Would the test be unfair to any class of citizens?

    d. Could such a test be easily incorporated into our laws?

6. *Resolved,* That vivisection should be prohibited.

    a. Is vivisection of great assistance to medicine?

    b. Is vivisection humane?

    c. Is it right for us as human beings to sanction the many forms of needless and excessive cruelty practised by vivisectors?

C. Make a brief introduction to each of the following propositions, defining all words that require definition, explaining the meaning of the proposition, stating the issues, and making the partition:—

1. All colleges should debar freshmen from participation in intercollegiate athletic contests.

2. Playing baseball with organizations not under the

Conviction in the Introduction

national agreement should not render athletes ineligible for college teams.

3. —— College should adopt the honor system of holding examinations.

4. All colleges should abolish hazing.

5. The climate of our country is changing.

6. Macbeth's wife was the cause of his ruin.

7. The Rhodes scholarships for the United States will accomplish the objects of its founder.

8. National expositions are a benefit to the country.

CHAPTER V

THE INTRODUCTION — BRIEF-DRAWING

PRECEDING chapters have dwelt on the essential characteristics of the introduction and have shown what it should be like when completed. No one but an expert writer, however, can hope that his argument, in either introduction, discussion, or conclusion, will attain any considerable completeness and excellence without first passing through a preliminary form known as the *brief*.

A brief is a special kind of outline: *it is an outline that sets forth in specific language all the ideas to be used in that portion of the argument known as conviction, and that shows the exact relation these ideas bear to each other and to the proposition.* An outline in narrative, descriptive, or expository composition is invariably made up of general suggestions, which seldom indicate the same ideas to different persons; it is inexact and incomplete. A brief, on the contrary, fails in its purpose unless it conveys accurate information. The material composing it is always in the form of complete sentences; the ideas are expressed in as exact and specific language as the writer is capable of using. A good brief means as much to the one who reads it as to the one who draws it. It is, too, a complete work in itself. It does not deal with persuasion; with this exception, however, it contains in condensed form all the material to be used in the finished argument.

There are many reasons why an arguer should first cast his material in the form of a brief. To begin with, this device enables him to grasp, almost at a glance, all the material used for the purpose of conviction; it keeps constantly before him the points that he must explain, and shows him instantly just how far he has progressed with the proof of each statement. Furthermore, a brief renders the arguer invaluable assistance in preserving the fundamental principles of composition, especially those of Unity, Coherence, Proportion, and Emphasis. It greatly simplifies his task of assorting material and assigning each part its proper place and function. It exhibits so clearly every particle of evidence and every process of reasoning employed that it affords great convenience for testing both the quality and the quantity of the proof. In fact, a good brief is so essential a part of a good argument that a student who neglects to draw the first is bound to meet failure in the second.

The rules governing brief-drawing logically divide themselves into four classes: those which apply to the brief as a whole constitute the first class and are called General Rules; those rules which apply to each of the main divisions of a brief constitute the three remaining classes and are called Rules for the Introduction, Rules for the Discussion, and Rules for the Conclusion.

GENERAL RULES.

In drawing a brief, the student should first divide his material into three groups, corresponding to the· three divisions of the complete argument: the Introduction, Discussion, and Conclusion. Moreover, since absolute clearness in every particular is the prime requisite for a good brief, he should label each of these parts with its proper name, so that there may never be the slightest doubt or confusion as to where one part ends and another begins. Hence the first rule for brief-drawing is:—

Rule I. *Divide the brief into three parts, and*

Brief of the Introduction

mark them respectively, Introduction, Discussion, and Conclusion.

A brief, as has been explained, is an outline that contains all the reasoning to be found in the finished argument.   Reasoning processes are carried on, not with vague ideas and general suggestions, but with specific facts and exact thoughts.   For this reason, only complete statements are of value in a brief. Mere terms must be avoided.   A statement, it should be remembered, is a declarative sentence; a term is a word or any combination of words other than a sentence.

The following examples of terms plainly show that no reasoning process can exist without the use of complete statements :—

Strikes during the past twenty-five years.

Percentage of strikes conducted by labor organizations.

Building trades and strikes.

Since such expressions as these give no information, they are manifestly out of place in a brief. Each term may call to mind any one of several ideas.   No one but the author knows whether the first term is intended to indicate that strikes have been of frequent or of infrequent occurrence, beneficial or detrimental.   The second term does not in-

Brief of the Introduction

dicate whether the percentage of strikes conducted by labor organizations has been great or small, increasing or decreasing. The third term is equally indefinite. Notice, however, that as soon as these terms are turned into complete sentences, they may well serve as explanation or as proof:—

During the twenty-five year period ending in 1905 there occurred in the United States 36,757 strikes.

Labor organizations directed about two-thirds of these strikes.

The building trades have had more strikes than has any other industry.

This explanation gives rise to the following rule:—

Rule II. *Express each idea in the brief in the form of a complete statement.*

Moreover, each sentence should contain only one idea. Every thought expressed has some specific work to do, and it can do it far more effectively if it stands by itself as a unit. The awkwardness and impracticability of proving the truth or falsity of a statement that makes several assertions has been treated under the head of Combined Propositions. Obviously, there are unwarrantable difficulties in grouping explanation or proof about such a statement as, " Municipal ownership has failed in Philadelphia, has succeeded in Edinburgh, and is likely to meet with indifferent success in New Orleans." Furthermore, a sentence that contains several distinct thoughts is very ineffective as proof for some other statement. Since one part of the sentence may be accepted as true and another part rejected, the resulting confusion is very great. To avoid all errors of this kind, the student should use, as far as possible, only *simple* sentences.

Rule III. *Make in each statement only a single assertion.*

In the next place, one who draws a brief should take pains to frame all his statements in as concise a form as he can. If he is able to state an idea in six words, he should not use seven. This principle does not mean that small words like *a, an,* and *the* should be left out, or that an obvious subject may be omitted; it does not mean that the "diary" style of writing is permissible. It means simply that one should always state his ideas as briefly as possible without violating any of the rules of Composition. Quotations should rarely appear in a brief, never unless they are very short. When an arguer wishes to make use of another writer's material, he should condense it into his own language, and state from what source he derived his information. In an expanded argument the full quotation may appear. The ability to express ideas both concisely and, at the same time, clearly, is attained only by considerable labor, yet a departure from the principle of brevity is a serious violation of good brief-drawing. Hence the rule :—

Rule IV. *Make each statement as concise as is consistent with clearness.*

Every brief is primarily a process of explanation. From this fact it is evident that clearness must be sought above all other qualities. Not only must the idea expressed be understood, but the *relation between* ideas, must be perfectly plain and evident. The reader should be able to see at a glance what material is of co-ordinate rank and what is of subordinate rank. This perspicuity is especially necessary in the discussion, where each statement is either being proved by subordinate statements or is serving as proof for some other statement. The device ordinarily adopted for exhibiting at a glance the relation between the ideas in a brief consists of two parts: first, all subordinate statements are indented farther than more important statements; and second, numbers and letters are used to indicate what statements are of co-ordinate importance and what are of secondary rank. The system of marking most generally adopted is as follows:—

Brief of the Introduction

I.

    A.

        1.

            a.

                1'.

                    a'.

    B.

        1.

            a.

II.

    A. etc.

Thus the fifth rule is:—

Rule V. *Indicate the relation between statements by indentation and by the use of symbols.*

In indicating the relation between ideas, a writer should never put more than one symbol before a statement. It seems almost superfluous to mention an error so apparent as the double use of symbols, but the mistake is frequently made and much confusion results. The numeral I before a heading indicates that the statement is of primary importance; the letter A indicates that it is of secondary importance. If a statement is marked IA, apparently it is both primary and secondary, clearly an impossibility.

Brief of the Introduction

Rule VI. *Mark each statement with only one symbol.*

RULES FOR THE INTRODUCTION.

It has been seen that a brief is a complete composition in itself, embodying all the material for conviction that will later be found in the expanded argument. The introduction, therefore, must contain sufficient information to make the proof of the proposition perfectly clear. This portion of the brief serves as a connecting link between the proposition and the discussion; it must explain the nature of the proposition and then show how the proof which is to follow applies to it. The exact work that the introduction to a brief must perform is stated in the following rule :—

Rule VII. *Put into the introduction sufficient explanation for a complete understanding of the discussion; this explanation usually involves :—*

      (a) *a definition of terms,*

      (b) *an explanation of the meaning of the proposition,*

      (c) *a statement of the issues, and*

      (d) *the partition.*

Neither an introduction to a brief nor an introduc-

Brief of the Introduction

tion to a complete argument should contain any statements not admitted by both sides. All ideas that savor of controversy or prejudice have no place in an introduction. The sole purpose of the introduction is to prepare the way for the discussion; if it contains anything in the nature of proof, anything which is not admittedly true, it is no longer pure introduction, but becomes in part discussion. If explanation and proof are thus thrown together indiscriminately, confusion will result. Accordingly the following rule is of great importance:—

Rule VIII. *Put into the introduction only statements admitted by both sides.*

The following introductions to briefs may well serve as models for student's work:—

FIRST MODEL.

Resolved, That England should permanently retain control of Egypt.

Negative Brief.

INTRODUCTION.

I. Because of the recent rapid development of Egypt, the question of the retention of this country is becoming important.

Brief of the Introduction

II. The following explanations will aid in the discussion of the problem:—

   A. Egypt is that strip of country in the northeastern part of Africa, drained by the Nile and its tributaries.

   B. England has an army of occupation in Egypt, and governs it nominally through the Khedive.

   C. England has never suggested annexation.

   D. England has shut out the interference of France and other European nations.

   E. England has practically ruled Egypt as a dependency.

III. The following facts are agreed upon:—

   A. Some nation had to take charge of Egypt, for

      1. The country was heavily in debt.

      2. The people were starving.

   B. It is for the advantage of England to retain control of the country.

IV. The conflicting arguments on the question are as follows:—

   A. Those who favor the control of Egypt by England have certain beliefs:—

Brief of the Introduction

B. They believe that the control of Egypt by England is the only practical solution of the problem.

2. They believe that the present status of affairs is beneficial to Egypt and to the whole world.

B. Those opposed to the control of Egypt by England maintain the following:—

1. They maintain that England rules in a selfish manner.

2. They maintain that Turkey and not England should have control of Egypt.

V. From this conflict of opinion it appears that the points to be determined are:—

A. Is Egypt benefited by the control of England?

B. Is the suzerainty of England over Egypt the only practical solution of the problem?

C. Is the control of Egypt by England a benefit to the whole world?

VI. The negative will attempt to prove that England should not permanently retain Egypt for the following reasons:

A. English control is harmful to Egypt.

Brief of the Introduction

B. English control is not the only solution to the Egyptian problem.

C. English control is harmful to other nations.

SECOND MODEL.

Resolved, That the President of the United States should be elected by direct popular vote.

Affirmative Brief.

INTRODUCTION.

I. The present method of electing the President of the United States has been both praised and condemned ever since the adoption of the Constitution.

    A. Two methods of electing the President are under consideration: the present system whereby the President is elected by the electoral college, and the proposed system whereby the President would be elected by a direct popular vote of the people.

II. These two systems may be described as follows:—

    A. The present system has the following characteristics:—

Brief of the Introduction

1. Each state elects a number of electors equal to the whole number of Senators and Representatives to which the state is entitled in Congress.

2. These electors are chosen as the Legislature of each state may direct.

3. The electors meet in their respective states and vote by ballot for the President.

4. Since the year 1800 the electors have always voted for the candidate nominated by the national party which elected them, though the Constitution does not make this requirement.

5. The ballots are sent in sealed packages to the President of the Senate, who counts them and declares the candidate receiving a majority vote elected.

6. If the electors fail to elect, the House of Representatives chooses a President from the three candidates that receive the greatest number of electoral votes.

Brief of the Introduction

B. The proposed system has the following characteristics:—

    1. The people vote directly for the President, the candidate receiving a majority of the votes being elected.

    2. If there be no majority, the President is elected as under the present system when the electors fail to elect.

III. The real question to be answered is, Should the direct method be substituted for the present method?

A. The comparative value of each method must be judged by the following standards:—

    1. Which would be the more practicable?

    2. Which would give the voter fuller enjoyment of his right of suffrage?

    3. Which method would have the better effect upon the general welfare of the nation?

IV. The affirmative will uphold its side of the proposition by establishing the three following facts:—

Brief of the Introduction

A. The direct popular vote system would be more practicable.

B. The direct popular vote system would be more democratic.

C. The direct popular vote system would be better for the general welfare of the nation.

EXERCISES.

A. (1) Criticise the following Introduction to a brief, and
   (2) Write a suitable Introduction to a brief on this subject.

City Location for College.

Introduction.

A. This question is important.
   1. The following explanation will aid —
   (a) In the understanding, and
   (b) In the discussion of the question.
      1. Primarily men come to college to study.
      2. Men can study better in the country.
      3. But is this really the case?
B. A college is an institution of learning higher in rank than a high school or an academy.
C. The issues of the question are the following:
   I. Which college location is more favorable to health and intellectual development?
   II. Is the student able to enter athletics?
   III. Does the student in the lonely country college form more lasting friendships?
   IV. Which is the cheaper?
   Which is the better location?

Brief of the Introduction

B. Put into brief form the Introduction found on page 44.

C. Put the following Introductions into brief form:—

(1) HOW TRUSTS AFFECT PRICES.

Perhaps no subject in connection with the Industrial Combinations of the last few years has been more discussed than that of their influence upon prices. Opinions have differed widely, the opponents of the Combinations usually believing that they have increased prices materially, their defenders claiming with equal positiveness that they have reduced prices. Differences of opinion have probably originated largely from the fact that the subject has been approached from different points of view; and mistakes have also, in many cases, been made through lack of a careful interpretation of available facts. It by no means follows that the Trusts have lowered prices because prices have fallen within a few years after their formation; nor, on the other hand, that Trusts have raised prices because prices have been increased. Neither does it follow that, because the Industrial Combinations might through their economies lower prices, they have, as a matter of fact, actually done so; nor again that, with the possible ability to increase prices through the exercise of monopolistic power, they have not found it advisable under certain circumstances really to lower them. Any careful discussion of the subject will involve, first, what the influence of combination would enable the Trusts to do regarding prices; second, what the Combinations actually have done; and, third, what effects upon society may be anticipated from any changes in prices made by Industrial Combinations.[1]

(2) Mr. Chairman: This bill (H. R. 17019) which I

[1] Jeremiah W. Jenks, North American Review for June, 1901, p. 906.

Brief of the Introduction

shall ask this House to pass to-day is one of that general class usually called "private bills"; and while the usage of this House might catalogue it under that head, it is in reality a "public bill," because it has to do with the interests of many people — indeed, an entire city of 75,000 population.

This bill provides that the legal title to a certain tract of land situated near the city of Tacoma, the title to which is now in the United States Government, shall be transferred to the city of Tacoma.

However, I wish to assure this House that as a matter of fact the Government practically loses nothing by the passage of this bill. I realize that these two statements placed side by side seem to involve a contradiction. Therefore I will make a brief explanation of this matter.

Since the year of 1866 the Government has owned a tract of land adjoining what is now the city of Tacoma; this tract of land contains 637.9 acres. In the year of 1888 the Government gave the city of Tacoma a right or license to use and occupy this land as a city park, but retained the legal title in the Government, because it was thought that at some future time the Government might need to use and occupy this land for military purposes. Therefore you will observe that the present condition of the title to this land is that the legal title is in the Government, with the right in the city to use and occupy the same. This bill, if it shall pass, will simply reverse and place the legal title to this land in the city of Tacoma, with the right remaining in the Government for all time to come to take possession or use and occupy any or all of this land that it might need for military, naval, or lighthouse purposes.

I wish to explain briefly to this House why the passage of this bill and this change in the title is not only fair and just, but the failure to pass this bill would, in my judgment, be very unfair to the 75,000 people in the city of Tacoma.[1]

(3) GOVERNMENT MANAGEMENT OF INDUS-TRIAL ENTERPRISES.[2]

By far the most important part of consumers' co-operation is exemplified in government management of industrial enterprises. This differs in two important particulars from the co-operative agencies already described. In the first place the choice of managers of a government business enterprise is connected with the general political machinery of the country, and regulated by constitutional law instead of by statutes of incorporation. In the second place, these managers are likely to fall back on the taxing powers of the Government to make up any deficit which may arise in the operations of a public business enterprise; or in the converse case to devote any surplus above expenses to the relief of tax burdens elsewhere. A government enterprise is managed by the people who represent, or are supposed to represent, the consumers; but the good or bad economy of its management does not necessarily redound to the profit or loss of those who most use it.

In the beginning of history, the government is the power that controls the army. When tribes were in a state of warfare with one another defense against foreign enemies was a matter of primary importance. No man could let his private convenience stand in the way of effective military operations. The discipline and subordination necessary to wage successful war were all-important; and all the powers necessary to maintain such discipline were entrusted to the leaders of the army.

Somewhat later the military authorities undertook the

---

[1] Speech of Hon. Francis W. Cushman of Washington, in the House of Representatives, Feb. 28, 1905.

[2] A. T. Hadley, *Economics,* pp. 390–393.

Brief of the Introduction

work of maintaining discipline in time of peace as well as war, and of defining and enforcing the rights of members of the tribe against one another, no less than against foreign enemies. This function was not accorded to them without a struggle. The priests, under whose tutelage the religious sanction for tribal customs had grown up, tried to keep in their own hands the responsibility of upholding these customs and the physical power connected with it. In some races they succeeded, but among European peoples the military authorities took the work of enforcing and defining laws out of the hands of the priests, and made it a function of the state as distinct from the Church. As security from foreign enemies increased, this law-making power became more and more important. The Government was less exclusively identified with the army, and more occupied with the courts, the legislatures, and the internal police. Its judicial and legislative functions assumed a prominence at least as great as its military function.

The growth of private property was also coincident with the development of these domestic functions of government. In fact, the two things reinforced one another. The production and accumulation of capital, to which private property gave so vigorous an impulse, placed the strong men of the community in a position where they had less to gain by war and more by peace. It put them on the side of internal tranquillity. It thus made the government more powerful, and this in turn still further increased the accumulations of capital. But along with this mutual help, which strong domestic government and strong property right rendered one another, there was an element of mutual antagonism. The very fulfillment of those functions which made the accumulation of capital possible, rendered it impossible for the government to do its work except at the expense of the capitalists. It was no longer possible to support armies by booty, or courts

Brief of the Introduction

by fines and forfeitures. The expense of maintaining order had to be paid by its friends instead of by its enemies. The growth of private property was followed by the development of a system of taxation, which, in theory at any rate, involved the power to destroy such property.

The existence of such a system of taxation, with the machinery for collecting money in this way, allows the government more freedom of industrial action than any private individual can command. It can make up a deficit by compulsory payments; and this gives it a wider range of power in deciding what services it will undertake and what prices it will charge — a power which affords almost unlimited opportunity for good or bad use, according to the degree of skill and integrity with which it is exercised.

Every extension of government activity into new fields restricts private enterprise in two ways: first by limiting the field for investment of private capital, and second, by possibly, if not probably, appropriating through taxation a part of the returns from private enterprise in all other fields. The question whether a government should manage an industry reduces itself to this: Are the deficiencies or evils connected with private management such that it is wise to give government officials the taxing power which constitutes the distinctive feature of public industrial management?

D. Draw an Introduction to a brief on each of the propositions given on page 82.

CHAPTER VI

THE DISCUSSION — CONVICTION

It has been seen that one who wishes to establish the truth or the falsity of a proposition must answer certain vital questions that are bound to arise in connection with it. Then, as different persons may answer these questions in different ways, it becomes necessary for him to convince his audience that his answers are correct. He must always beware of assertiveness. This defect occurs whenever a speaker or writer makes a statement but does not establish its truth. As simple denial is always sufficient answer to mere assertion, an unsupported statement is worthless. No one can hope to win in debate or change another's belief unless he can prove that what he says is true; he must substantiate with proof every statement that he makes, and show that no possibility for error or deceit can exist. *In argumentation every statement not commonly accepted as true must be proved.*

The Discussion

The following passage is a highly assertive bit of argument; its worthlessness is apparent.

The decision of Congress to increase still further our already enormous navy is an injustice to every individual who contributes to the support of the national government. It is a crime to squander millions of money on a fleet that we do not need. Our navy to-day is more than the equal of any foreign armament that floats. Though second in number of ships, it ranks first in efficiency among all the navies of the world. No other country can boast of such marksmanship as our gunners display; no other country can boast of such armor plate as is to be found on our first-class battleships; not even England can successfully compete with us in seamanship and in general efficiency.

Proof is " anything which serves either immediately or mediately to convince the mind of the truth or the falsehood of a fact or proposition." [1] Belief in a specific statement is induced by a presentation of pertinent facts, and usually by a process of reasoning whereby from the existence of these known facts, the conclusion, hitherto unaccepted, is reached. Those facts that have to do with the proposition under discussion are known as *evidence*. The process of combining facts and deriving an inference from them is known as *reasoning*. Evidence may be made up of the testimony of witnesses,

[1] On Evidence, Best, p. 45.

The Discussion

the opinion of experts, knowledge derived from experience, the testimony of documents, or circumstances that are generally known to have existed. Reasoning is the process by which men form opinions, render judgments, explain events, or in any way seek new truths from established facts.

In the following bit of proof, notice the facts that are stated, and see how, by a process of reasoning, they go to substantiate the idea that they are intended to prove:—

New York hires two policemen where Nashville hires one, and pays them double the salary; yet Nashville is as peaceable and orderly as New York. In Nashville any child of school age can have a seat in the public schools all through the year; in New York there has been a shortage of seats for many years. Nashville has a filtered water supply; New York is going to have one as soon as the $12,000,000 filtration plant can be built at Jerome Park. Street car fares are five cents in both cities; in Nashville one can always get a seat; in New York one has to scramble for standing room. The southern city maintains hospitals, parks, food inspectors, and all other things common to New York and other large cities. Apparently, Nashville is giving as much to its inhabitants for six dollars per capita as New York for thirty-one. These facts can point to but one conclusion — that Nashville has a superior system of government.

Since the first step in the generation of proof is the discovery of facts, the arguer should at the very outset become sufficiently familiar with the various

kinds of evidence to estimate the value and strength
of each idea that has a bearing upon the subject.

I. EVIDENCE.

There are two kinds of evidence: (a) direct, and
(b) indirect or circumstantial. If a man sees a
gang of strikers set fire to the buildings of their
former employer, his evidence is direct. If, however, he only sees them stealthily leaving the buildings just before the fire breaks out, his evidence is
indirect. In the latter case the man's testimony is
direct evidence that the men were in the vicinity of
the fire when it started, but it is indirect evidence
that they perpetrated the crime. If a student who
has failed to do good work throughout the term,
and who has had little or no opportunity for special
preparation, passes in a perfect paper at the close
of an examination, the presumption is that he has
received aid. The evidence on which this supposition rests is entirely circumstantial. But if some
one saw the student obtaining aid, that fact would
be direct evidence against him.

Direct evidence, as a rule, is considered more
valuable than indirect, but each kind is frequently
sufficient to induce belief. The best possible kind

The Discussion

of evidence, the kind that is least liable to contain error or falsehood, is a combination of both direct and indirect. Either one by itself may be untrustworthy. The unreliability of evidence given by eyewitnesses is shown by the conflicting stories they frequently tell concerning the same incident even when they are honestly attempting to relate the facts as they occurred. Also, it is always possible that the inferences drawn from a combination of circumstances may be entirely wrong. When, however, both kinds of evidence are available, each confirming the other and leading up to the same conclusion, then the possibility of error is reduced to a minimum.

The opportunity of the college student for obtaining evidence in his argumentative work is limited. A lawyer before entering upon an important case often spends weeks and months in investigation; scientists sometimes devote a whole lifetime in trying to establish a single hypothesis. But the college student in preparing an argument must obtain his evidence in a few days. There are several sources at his disposal. The first available source is his fund of general knowledge and experience. If a man can establish a statement by saying that he personally knows it to be true, he has valuable proof. Then the people with whom the student comes in contact constitute another source of evidence. Anyone who can give information on a subject that is being investigated is a valuable witness. Especially in discussions on questions which pertain to college life, the opinions and experiences of college men and of prominent educators are unsurpassed as evidence. But the greatest source of evidence for the student of argumentation is the library. Here he may consult the best thought of all time in every branch of activity. He may review the opinions of statesmen, economists, educators, and scientists, and introduce as evidence their experiences and the results of their investigations. Here he may familiarize himself with the current events of the world, and draw his own conclusions as to their significance. In fact, a well equipped library treats of all subjects, however broad or narrow they may be, and furnishes evidence for all sorts of debatable questions.

As not all evidence is equally valuable, a large part of the work of argumentation consists in applying tests to the evidence at hand for the sake of determining what facts are irrefutable, what are doubtful, and what are worthless. Moreover, one engaged in argumentation must test not only his

The Discussion

own evidence but also that of the other side. No better method of refuting an opponent's argument exists than to show that the facts on which it rests are untrustworthy. Tests of evidence may be divided into two classes: tests of the source from which it comes, and tests of the quality of the evidence itself.

A. Tests of the Source of Evidence.

Since in courts of law, in college debate, and in all kinds of argumentation, facts are established by the testimony of witnesses, the sources of evidence are the witnesses who give it. The debater and the argumentative writer have not the opportunity, as has the lawyer, of producing the witnesses and permitting them to tell their own stories to the audience. He must himself relate the evidence; and, in order that it may be believed, he must tell whence it comes. The sources of evidence may be common rumor, newspapers, magazines, official documents, private citizens, or public officials. The extent to which these witnesses are accepted as trustworthy by the people before whom they are quoted determines in a large measure whether or not the evidence will be believed. Tests for determining the trustworthiness of witnesses will next be given.

The Discussion

The first test of the source of evidence should be :—

(1) *Is the witness competent to give a trustworthy account of the matter under consideration?*

To answer this question, first determine whether the facts to be established are such that any ordinary person can speak concerning them with reasonable accuracy, or whether they can be understood only by persons who have received special training. A landsman could well testify that a naval battle had occurred, but only a man with nautical training could accurately describe the maneuvers of the ships and tell just how the engagement progressed. A coal heaver's description of a surgical operation would establish nothing, except perhaps the identity of the people and a few other general matters; only a person with a medical education could accurately describe the procedure. The testimony of any one but a naturalist would not even tend to prove the existence of an hitherto unknown species of animal life. A witness without technical knowledge cannot give reliable evidence on matters of a technical nature.

Then, if it is found that the witness does possess the necessary technical training, or that no previous training is necessary, still further test his ability to

The Discussion

give reliable evidence by asking whether he has had
ample opportunity for investigating the facts to the
existence of which he testifies. For even a skilled
player sitting in the first base bleachers at a baseball
game to criticise an umpire's decisions on balls and
strikes is absurd; the opinion of a transient visitor
to Panama on the methods used in digging the
canal is not valuable; a traveler who has spent a
single month in Japan cannot draw reliable conclusions on the merits and defects of its political
structure. In not one of these cases has the opportunity for investigation been sufficient to render
the witness able to give reliable evidence.

A current magazine in discussing the weakness of
testimony that comes from incompetent witnesses
says :—

Generalizations about the tastes and interests of the age
are so easy that all except the most wary fall into them,
and the world is full of off-hand opinions touching the
condition of society and the state of the world, which
are far more conspicuous for courage than for discretion.
There are very few men or women in any particular
period who know it intimately enough, and with sufficient
insight and sympathy, to pass judgment upon it. One
hears almost every day sweeping judgments about Americans, English, French, Germans, Chinese, and Japanese
which are entirely valueless, unless they are based on a
very broad and intimate knowledge of these various
peoples, a knowledge which, in the nature of things, few

The Discussion

people possess. The charming American girl who declared that, since gloves are cheaper in Paris, American civilization is a failure, may stand for a type of interesting and piquant oracles, to be heard with attention, but under no circumstances to be followed. Americans are so familiar with the European traveler who arrives and makes up his opinion over night in regard to men, morals, and manners in the Western world and have so often been the victim of this self-confident critic, that they ought not to repeat the same blunder in dealing with other peoples.[1]

In the court room, where witnesses are present and can be carefully examined by the lawyers on both sides, it is customary to apply both mental and physical tests. The witness who testifies to knowledge of some event that occurred a long time before is given a memory test; the senses, also, through which occurrences are perceived are frequently examined. But as writers and debaters in general seldom have the opportunity to apply tests of this sort to their sources of information, and as these tests are seldom important outside of the law courts, they are not taken up in detail in this book.

The second test of the source of evidence should be :—

(2)   *Is the witness willing to give an accurate account of the matter?*

One important influence that may cause a witness

[1] The Outlook, July 20, 1907.

114

The Discussion

to give false evidence is *self-interest*. Not only individuals, but social and industrial organizations, political parties, communities, and states are frequently swayed by this emotion to the extent of deliberately perverting the truth. The evidence found in newspapers and other publications is often false, or at least misleading, because it has been tampered with by those who put their selfish interests before all else. The owner of an industry protected by a high tariff would scarcely be considered a reliable witness in matters affecting tariff reform. The opinion of a railroad magnate on the subject of a compulsory two-cent rate law would not be considered as unbiased. No disinterested seeker after truth would accept the political conclusions of a newspaper owned by a politician or recognized as the organ of a certain party. In all such cases, self-interest may prompt the witness to make statements not in strict accordance with the truth. Perjury in the court room is not uncommon; falsehood elsewhere must be guarded against. The arguer should always carefully scrutinize the testimony of a witness that has any special interest in the matter for which evidence is being sought. Though the self-interest is strong, the witness may be willing to state the matter accurately; but, as long as human nature remains as it is, this willingness should not be taken for granted.

The third test of the source of evidence should be :—

(3) *Is the witness prejudiced?*

Another emotion that frequently keeps a witness from telling the exact truth is *prejudice*. Every one is familiar with instances of how this passion warps men's morals and corrupts their judgment. If a man is prejudiced for or against a person or a system, he cannot be accepted as a trustworthy witness in matters where his prejudice comes into play. Should an economist known to favor socialism write a treatise advocating municipal ownership of public utilities, his evidence and his reasoning would not be convincing; it would be taken for granted that he looked at the subject through socialistic spectacles. A person who sets out with the expectation and intention of finding flaws in anything usually succeeds. Though he is willing to tell the exact truth, yet because of his prejudice he is sure to see only that which will coincide with his preconceived opinions. For this reason, political speeches and intensely partisan books and papers are invariably unreliable sources of evidence even though they are not intentionally dishonest.

The Discussion

The fourth test of the source of evidence is:—

(4) *Does the witness have a good reputation for honesty and accuracy?*

The human conscience is so constituted that many people deviate from the truth for no apparent reason whatever. Some are given to exaggeration; some habitually pretend to know that of which they are entirely ignorant; others are so inaccurate that everything they say is open to grave suspicion. If a witness is known to have been repeatedly dishonest or inaccurate in the past, little reliance should be placed in his testimony. " Yellow journalism," which is largely the reflection of common rumor, affords constant examples of witnesses that give questionable evidence.

Ability and willingness to give exact evidence, an unprejudiced attitude, and a good reputation for honesty and accuracy are the qualities that should characterize the sources of evidence. If a writer or speaker is securing testimony from friends or acquaintances, the application of these tests is not difficult. If, however, the sources are books and periodicals, his work is harder; but to be successful, he must not shirk it. When one procures evidence from books, he should investigate the character and standing of the author. When one obtains it from signed articles in papers and magazines, he must consider both the author and the character of the publication. In the case of newspaper " stories " and editorials, one should find out on what general policy and principles the paper is conducted. A cautious arguer will always avoid, as far as he can, the use of evidence that comes from a doubtful source. If one finds that an opponent has used the testimony of questionable witnesses, he can, by exposing the fact, easily refute the argument.

Necessity of stating sources. It sometimes happens that an arguer fails to state the source of his evidence. This omission is usually fatal to success. No one is likely to put much confidence in statements that are introduced by such flimsy preambles as, " A certain statesman has declared "; " I have read somewhere "; " An acquaintance told me." Not only must evidence come from sources that seem good to the writer, but those sources must be satisfactory to the audience. In the last analysis the audience is the judge of what is credible and what is not. Moreover, if the evidence is of great importance, or is liable to be disputed, the arguer should show in a few words why the witness is especially reliable.

The Discussion

B. Internal Tests of Evidence.

(1) *Is the evidence consistent with (a) other evidence in the same argument; (b) known facts; (c) human experience?*

The requirement that every separate bit of evidence in an argument shall be consistent with every other bit of evidence in the same argument is too well understood to need explanation. One familiar with courts of law knows that a witness who contradicts himself is not believed. Furthermore, if the testimony of several witnesses for the same side is inconsistent, the case for that side is materially weakened. So it is in general debate: the arguer who wishes to succeed must not use evidence that is self-contradictory. His proof must "hang together"; his facts must all go to establish the same conclusion.

A flagrant violation of this principle once occurred in a class-room debate. The speaker for the negative on the proposition, "*Resolved,* That freshmen should be ineligible for college teams," said that such a rule would deprive the freshmen of much-needed physical exercise. Later on, he said that just as many freshmen would receive injuries under this rule as without it, since they would take part in equally dangerous contests as members of freshmen teams. This contradiction ruined his argument.

In the next place, evidence to be of any value whatever, must be consistent with what is known about the case. If an arguer is so careless as to make statements contradictory either to well-established facts or to facts easily proved, he cannot hope to attain the slightest measure of success. Only one guilty of gross neglect or absolute falsehood is likely to fall into such an error. At one time the story was circulated that, during his early life, Lincoln had been insane. In the following passage Ida M. Tarbell shows that the testimony on which this belief was founded is inconsistent with the known facts of the case, and is, therefore, palpably untrue :—

"Mr. Thornton went on to say that he knew beyond a doubt that the sensational account of Lincoln's insanity was untrue, and he quoted from the House journal to show how it was impossible that, as Lamon says, using Herndon's notes, 'Lincoln went crazy as a loon, and did not attend the legislature in 1841–1842, for this reason'; or, as Herndon says, that he had to be watched constantly. According to the record taken from the journals of the House by Mr. Thornton, which have been verified in Springfield, Mr. Lincoln was in his seat in the House on that 'fatal first of January' when he is asserted to have

The Discussion

been groping in the shadow of madness, and he was also there on the following day."

Lincoln himself was an expert at detecting inconsistency wherever it existed. He won many of his lawsuits by the straightforward method of showing that the one or two vital statements on which the whole case of the opposition rested were false, inasmuch as they were inconsistent with well-established and incontrovertible facts. An instance of this sort is here described:—

The most damaging evidence was that of one Allen, who swore that he had seen Armstrong strike Metzker about ten or eleven o'clock in the evening. When asked how he could see, he answered that the moon shone brightly. Under Lincoln's questioning he repeated the statement until it was impossible that the jury should forget it. With Allen's testimony unimpeached, conviction seemed certain.

Lincoln's address to the jury was full of pathos. It was not as a hired attorney that he was there, he said, but to discharge a debt of friendship. . . . But Lincoln was not relying on sympathy alone to win his case. In closing he reviewed the evidence, showing that all depended on Allen's testimony, and this he said he could prove to be false. Allen never saw Armstrong strike Metzker by the light of the moon, for at the hour when he said he saw the fight, between ten and eleven o'clock, the moon was not in the heavens. Then procuring an almanac, he passed it to the judge and jury. The moon, which was on that night only in its first quarter, had set before midnight.[1]

An arguer should also be extremely careful to use evidence that on its face appears reasonable. Only an extremely credulous audience will accept ideas that run counter to human belief and experience. To attribute the occurrence of an event to supernatural causes would bring a smile of derision to any but a most ignorant and superstitious person. To attribute to men qualities and characteristics that human experience has shown they do not possess will bring equal discredit. No one is likely to accept evidence that contradicts his habits of thinking, that is contrary to what his life and experience have taught him is true. For this reason savage people are slow to believe the teachings of the Christian religion. For this reason it is difficult to make an audience believe that any one will deliberately and consistently work against his own interests, or follow any other unusual line of action. Evidence contrary to human experience may be true, but unless the exigencies of the argument demand its use, the arguer will do well to omit it entirely. If he is obliged to use it, he should make

[1] The Life of Abraham Lincoln, Vol. I, p. 272. Ida M. Tarbell. The Doubleday & McClure Co.

The Discussion

it appear as reasonable as he can, and also substantiate it with careful proof.

Huxley appreciated the fact that evidence, to be believed, must be in accordance with man's experience when he wrote the following:—

> If any one were to try to persuade you that an oyster shell (which is also chiefly composed of carbonate of lime) had crystallized out of sea-water, I suppose you would laugh at the absurdity. Your laughter would be justified by the fact that all experience tends to show that oyster-shells are formed by the agency of oysters, and in no other way.

The ease with which an argument that does not satisfy this requirement may be overthrown is clearly shown in the following extract from a student's forensic:—

> To say that the Cuban reconcentrados sunk the *Maine* in an effort to embroil the United States in a conflict with Spain is the veriest foolishness. There is not one scrap of documentary evidence to show that such was the case. Moreover, such an act would be unparalleled in the annals of history. It is unreasonable, contrary to all experience, that those oppressed people should have brought disaster, involving the destruction of property and the loss of many lives, upon the very nation that they were looking to for assistance.

(2) *Is the evidence first-hand or hearsay evidence?*

The Discussion

It is universally recognized that hearsay evidence is unreliable. A narrative is sure to become so garbled by passing from mouth to mouth that unless a witness can testify to a fact from his own personal knowledge the evidence he gives is worthy of little credence. There is sufficient chance for error when the person who witnessed the event relates the account himself; if the story is told by a second, and perhaps by a third person, it is likely to reflect but little of what really happened. Every one is familiar with the exaggerations of common rumor; it distorts facts so that they are unrecognizable. The works of Herodotus are untrustworthy because he frequently believed hearsay evidence. Since second-hand evidence both fails to establish anything worth while, if allowed to stand, and is easily overthrown even by a very little first-hand evidence, an arguer will do well to follow the custom of the law courts, and, as a rule, exclude it altogether.

(3) *Can the evidence be considered as especially valuable?*

(a) *Hurtful admissions* constitute an especially valuable kind of evidence. Since men are not wont to give evidence detrimental to their personal interest unless impelled to do so by conscientious scruples, any testimony damaging to the one who gives it is in all probability not only truthful, but also the result of careful investigation. When a practising physician admits that half the ailments of mankind are imaginary or so trivial as to need no medical attention, he is making a statement that is likely to injure his business; for this reason he is probably stating the result of his experience truthfully. If a railroad president says that in his opinion government supervision of railroads will benefit the public in the matter of rates and service, it may be taken for granted that he has given his honest belief, and that his natural reluctance to surrender any authority of his own has kept him from speaking carelessly. If a member of the United States Senate admits that that body is corrupt, and selfish, and untrustworthy, he is lowering his own rank; therefore it is reasonable to believe that he is speaking the truth according to his honest belief.

The following is an example of this kind of evidence:—

It was stated during the Manchurian campaign that the Jewish soldiers, of whom Kuropatkin had about 35,000, not only failed to hold their ground under fire, but by their timidity threw their comrades into panic. But good evidence can be cited from the correspondents of the

The Discussion

Novoye Vremya, an Anti-Semitic organ, to the effect that among the Jews were found many "intrepid and intelligent soldiers," and that a number of them were awarded the St. George's cross for gallantry.[1]

It is hardly necessary to add that one who places especial reliance on this kind of evidence must be sure that the admission is *really* and not merely *apparently* contrary to the interest of the one who gives it.

(b)   Another particularly valuable kind of evidence is *negative evidence,* or the *evidence of silence.* Whenever a witness fails to mention an event which, if it had occurred, would have been of such interest to him that he might reasonably have been expected to have mentioned it, his silence upon the matter becomes negative evidence that the event did not occur.   For many years no one suggested that Bacon wrote the Shakespearean plays; this absence of testimony to the belief that Bacon wrote them is strong evidence that such belief did not exist until recently, a fact that tends to discredit the Baconian theory of authorship.   The fact that in the writings of Dickens and Thackeray no mention is made of the bicycle is negative evidence that the bicycle had not then come into use.   That Moses nowhere in

[1] The Nation, June 11, 1908.

his writings speaks of life after death is negative evidence that the Hebrews did not believe in the immortality of the soul. If admittedly capable and impartial officials do not inflict penalties for foul playing during a football game, there is strong presumption that little or no foul playing occurred.

The following paragraph, taken from a current magazine, shows how this kind of evidence may be handled very effectively :—

A sharp controversy has been raging in the European press over the question whether Gambetta secretly visited Bismarck in 1878. Francis Laur, Gambetta's literary executor, has published an article asserting that he did, and giving details (rather vague, it must be admitted) of the conversation between the two statesmen. But he offers not a scrap of documentary proof. He is not even sure whether the interview took place at Friedrichsruh or at Varzin. This is rather disconcerting, especially in view of the fact that Bismarck never made the slightest reference in his reminiscences or letters to the visit of Gambetta, if it occurred, and that the minute Busch never mentioned it.[1]

C. Argument From Authority.

There is a particular kind of evidence frequently available for debaters and argumentative writers known as *argument from authority*. This evidence consists of the opinions and decisions of men who

[1] The Nation, September 5, 1907.

The Discussion

are recognized, to some extent at least, as authorities on the subjects of which they speak. An eminent scientist might explain with unquestioned certainty the operation of certain natural phenomena. A business man of wide experience and with well recognized insight into national conditions might speak authoritatively on the causes of business depressions. In religious matters the Bible is the highest authority for orthodox Christians; the Koran, for Mohammedans. In legal affairs the highest authorities are court decisions, opinions of eminent jurists, and the Constitution. If a certain college president is considered an authority in the matter of college discipline, then a quotation from him on the evils of hazing becomes valuable evidence for the affirmative of the proposition, " Hazing should be abolished in all colleges." If the arguer wishes to strengthen his evidence, he may do so by giving the president's reasons for condemning hazing; but he then departs from pure argument from authority. Pure argument from authority does not consist of a statement of the reasons involved; it asserts that something is true because some one who is acknowledged to be an authority on that subject says it is true.

Argument from authority differs from other

The Discussion

evidence in that it involves not merely investigation but also the exercise of a high degree of judgment. The statement that in 1902, in the United Kingdom, two hundred and ninety-five communities of from 8,000 to 25,000 inhabitants were without street-car lines is not argument from authority; the discovery of this truth involved merely investigation. On the other hand, if some reputable statesman or business man should say that street-car facilities in the United States excelled those of England, this evidence would be argument from authority; only through both investigation and judgment could such a statement be evolved.

This kind of evidence is very strong when those addressed have confidence in the integrity, ability, and judgment of the person quoted. If, however, they do not know him, or if they do not consider him reliable, the evidence is of little value. Therefore, the test that an arguer should apply before using this kind of evidence is as follows:—

Is the witness an acknowledged authority on the subject about which he speaks?

Sometimes a short statement showing why the witness quoted is able to speak wisely and conclusively will render the evidence more valuable in the eyes of the audience. In the following

9

The Discussion

example, notice how Judge James H. Blount used "authority" in proving that the Filipinos desired self-government:—

Senator Dubois, of Idaho, who was a member of the Congressional party that visited the Philippines, has since said in the New York "Independent": All the Filipinos, with the exception of those who were holding positions under and drawing salaries from our Government, favor a government of their own. There is scarcely an exception among them. . . . There is nobody in the islands, no organization of any kind or description, which favors the policy of our Government toward them.

Senator Newlands, of Nevada, also a member of the Congressional party aforesaid, has declared, in the number of this Review for December, 1905, that practically the whole people desire independence. Congressman Parsons, also a member of the same party, has since said: "There is no question that all the Filipino parties are now in favor of independence."

Captain J. A. Moss, of the Twenty-fourth Infantry, a member of General Corbin's staff, is quoted by Mr. Bryan, in the "Commoner" of April 27th, 1906, as saying in an article published in a Manila paper while Mr. Bryan was in the islands, with reference to the wishes of "the great majority" of Filipinos, that "to please them, we cannot get out of the islands too soon." [1]

II. REASONING.

As has been said, proof consists of evidence and reasoning. Evidence has been considered first be-

[1] North American Review, Vol. CLXXXIV, p. 136.

The Discussion

cause this order corresponds to the way in which proof is usually generated; obviously, the discovery of facts precedes the process of reasoning which shows their significance. In some instances, however, this order is reversed: a man may form a theory and then hunt for the facts on which to base it; but in general, facts precede inferences.

Since all people when they reason do not reach the same conclusion, it is very essential for a student to investigate the various processes of reasoning. Given exactly the same evidence, some men will draw one conclusion, some another. A current periodical recognizes this fact when it says:—

How widely divergent may be conclusions drawn from the same source can be judged by contrasting these two statements: Messrs. Clark and Edgar declare that "where municipal ownership has been removed from the realm of philosophic discussion and put to the test of actual experience it has failed ingloriously"; Professor Parsons and Mr. Bemis on the contrary assert, to use Professor Parsons' words, "it is not public ownership, but private ownership, that is responsible for our periodic crisis and the ruin of our industries," and "it is not impossible that the elimination of the public service corporations through public ownership is one of the things that would do more to help along the process of making our cities fit." [1]

Because of the divergencies in the results produced by reasoning, a student should study with

[1] The Outlook, July 27, 1907.

The Discussion

considerable care the various processes of arriving at a conclusion, so that he may be able to tell what methods are strong, what are weak, and what are fallacious.

According to a common classification, there are two methods of reasoning: the inductive process, and the deductive process.

1. **Inductive Reasoning.** When one carefully investigates his reasons for believing as he does, he often finds that he accepts a certain statement as true because he is familiar with many specific instances that tend to establish its truth. The belief that prussic acid is poisonous is based upon the large number of instances in which its deadly effect has been apparent. The fact that railroad men are exposed to injury is unquestioned because every one is familiar with the many accidents that occur each year. The statement that water freezes at thirty-two degrees Fahrenheit has been proved true by innumerable tests. This process of reasoning by which, from many specific instances, the truth of a general statement is established, is called *induction*.

An example of inductive reasoning is found in the following passage:—

The Discussion

Does the closing of the saloons affect appreciably the amount of drunkenness in the community? A comparison of the same town or city in successive years — one year under one system, and the next year under the other — furnishes a basis for accurate judgment. Evidence of this sort is all one way, and it seems to be conclusive.

The tables prepared by the Massachusetts Bureau of Statistics of Labor, in 1905, under special instructions from the legislature, show that in Haverhill the average number of arrests per month under license was 81.63, under no-license, 26.50; in Lynn, under license, 315, under no-license, 117.63; in Medford, under license, 20.12, under no-license, 13.25; in Pittsfield, under license, 93.25, under no-license, 36.75; and in Salem, under license, 140.50, under no-license, 29.63. Such comparisons might be multiplied, but it is unnecessary. There is no escaping the conclusion that the closing of the saloons, under the Local Option system, does sensibly diminish the volume of drunkenness.[1]

In using inductive reasoning, one must always be on his guard against drawing conclusions too hastily. It is never correct to conclude from a consideration of only a few instances that a general truth has been discovered. Further examination may show that the opinion first formed will not hold. Some people call all men dishonest because several acquaintances have not kept faith with them. Others are ready to believe that because they have made money in the stock market all can do likewise.

[1] Atlantic Monthly, Vol. XC, p. 437.

133

The Discussion

Most superstitions arise through generalization from too few instances: those who have several times met misfortune on the thirteenth day of the month are apt to say that the thirteenth is always an unlucky day. Such reasoning as this shows the weakness of inductive argument: a conclusion is worthless if it is drawn from too few examples.

Professor Fred Lewis Pattee, in writing on *Errors in Reasoning,* says:—

Children and even adults often generalize from a single experience. A little boy cautioned me at one time to keep away from a certain horse, for "white horses always kick." An old Pennsylvania farmer laid down the law that shingles laid during the increase of the moon always curl up. He had tried it once and found out. A friend will advise you to take Blank's Bitters: "I took a bottle one spring and felt much better; they always cure." Physicians base their knowledge of medicines upon the observations of thousands of trained observers through many years, and not upon a single experience. Most people are prone to judge their neighbors from too slight acquaintance. If a man is late at an appointment twice in succession, someone is sure to say: "Oh, he's always late." This is poor thinking because it is bad judgment. Judgments should be made with care and from fullness of experience.[1]

The following quotation illustrates how often

[1] The Adult Bible Class and Teacher Training Monthly, May, 1908, page 295.

The Discussion

hasty generalizations create prejudice and sway public judgment:—

There is an impression shared by many that the relation between the white and black races in this country is becoming less amicable and more and more surcharged with injustice. The basis for this impression is to be found in certain dramatic and sensational events, in particular the riots in Springfield, Illinois, and in Atlanta, Georgia. The memory of those events is becoming faint in many minds; but the impression they created remains. A dramatic event will have an effect upon public opinion which statistics, more significant but less picturesque, will altogether fail to produce. In the horror at the brief work of a mob the diminution in the annual number of lynchings is forgotten.

The fundamental mistake in this is in the picking out of a startling episode or a reckless utterance and regarding it as typical. We do not arrive at the truth in that way. The Black Hand assassin does not furnish a true index to the Italian character. Aaron Burr is not an exhibit of the product of American Puritanism. So, if we wish to find out what American democracy has done with the negro, we do not search, if we are wise, into the chain-gang of Georgia or into the slums of New York.[1]

The value of inductive reasoning depends upon the number of instances observed. Very seldom is it possible to investigate every case of the class under discussion. Of course this can sometimes be done. For instance, one may be able to state that

[1] The Outlook, April 4, 1908.

all his brothers are college graduates, since he can speak authoritatively concerning each one of them. But usually an examination of every instance is out of the question, and whenever induction is based on less than all existing cases, it establishes only *probable* truth.

From the foregoing it is seen that the tests for induction are two:—

(1) *Have enough instances of the class under consideration been investigated to establish the existence of a general law?*

(2) *Have enough instances been investigated to establish the probable existence of a general law?*

2. Deductive reasoning. Deductive reasoning is the method of demonstrating the truth of a particular statement by showing that some general principle, which has previously been established or which is admitted to be true, applies to it. A stranger on coming to the United States might ask whether our postal system is a success. The answer would perhaps be, " Yes, certainly it is, for it is maintained by the government, and all our government enterprises are successful." When the metal thurium was discovered, a query doubtless arose as to whether it was fusible. It was then reasoned that since all metals hitherto known were

The Discussion

fusible, and since thurium was a metal, undoubtedly it was fusible. Stated in clearer form, the reasoning in each case would be:—

A. All our government enterprises are successful.

B. The United States postal system is a government enterprise.

C. Therefore the United States postal system is successful.

A. All metals are fusible.

B. Thurium is a metal.

C. Therefore thurium is fusible.

Such a series of statements is called a syllogism. A syllogism always consists of a major premise (A), a minor premise (B), and a conclusion (C). The major premise always states a general law; the minor premise shows that the general law applies to the particular case under consideration; and the conclusion is, in the light of the two premises, an established truth.

The strength of deductive argument depends on two things: the truth of the premises and the framing of the syllogism. The syllogism must always be so stated that a conclusion is derived from the application of a general law to some specific instance to which the law obviously applies. In the next place, the premises must be true. If they are only probably correct, the conclusion is a mere presumption; if either one is false, the conclusion is probably false. But if the syllogism is correctly framed, and if both premises are true, the conclusion is irrefutable. As premises are facts that have first been established by induction, the relation between inductive and deductive reasoning is very close. In fact, deduction depends on induction for its very existence. To overthrow a deductive argument all that is necessary is to show the error in the inductive process that built up either one or both of the premises.

The tests for deduction are:—

(1) *Are both premises true?*

(2) *Is the fact stated in the minor premise an instance of the general law expressed in the major premise?*

In practical argumentation it is not always necessary or desirable to express a deductive argument in full syllogistic form. One premise is frequently omitted; the syllogism thus shortened is called an *enthymeme*. The reasoning then takes some such form as, " This man will fail in business because he is incompetent." The major premise, " All incompetent men fail in business," is understood, but

The Discussion

is not expressed. The enthymeme constitutes as strong and forceful an argument as the syllogism, provided the suppressed premise is a well-established fact; but whenever this premise is not accepted as true, it must be stated and proved. The argument will then consist of the full syllogistic process.

The following outline illustrates the chief difference between induction and deduction:—

The game of football benefits the players physically, because

(Induction.)

1. Football is known to have benefited Henry Harvey.
2. Football is known to have benefited Frank Barrs.
3. Football is known to have benefited Penn Armstrong.

(Deduction.)

1. The game affords the players regular exercise.
2. The game takes them out in the open air.
3. The game develops the lungs.

The deductive reasoning expressed in full would be :—

(1) A. All games that afford the players regular exercise benefit them physically.
B. Football affords the players regular exercise.
C. Therefore football benefits the players physically.

The reasoning given in (2) and (3) may be expressed in similar syllogisms.

The Discussion

To test the inductive part of this argument, one should determine how well the three examples show the existence of a general law. To test the deductive part, he should ask whether the premises, both those stated and those suppressed, are admitted facts, or whether they need to be proved.

If all reasoning were purely inductive or purely deductive, and if it always appeared in as simple a form as in the preceding illustration, one would have little difficulty in classifying and testing it. But frequently the two kinds appear in such obscure form and in such varied combinations that only an expert logician can separate and classify them. Because of this difficulty, it is worth while to know a second method of classification, one which is often of greater practical service than the method already discussed in assisting the arguer to determine what methods of reasoning are strong and what are weak. A knowledge of this classification is also very helpful to one who is searching for ways in which to generate proof. This method considers proof from the standpoint of its use in practical argument; it teaches not so much the different ways in which the mind may work, as the ways in which it must work to arrive at a sound conclusion.

The Discussion

1. ARGUMENT FROM ANTECEDENT PROBABILITY.

The process of reasoning from cause to effect is known as the argument from antecedent probability. Whenever a thinking man is asked to believe a statement, he is much readier to accept it as true if some reasonable *cause* is assigned for the existence of the fact that is being established. The argument from antecedent probability supplies this cause. The reasoning may be from the past toward the present, or from the present toward the future. If an inspector condemns a bridge as unsafe, the question arises, "What has made it so?" If some one prophesies a rise in the price of railroad bonds, he is not likely to be believed unless he can show an adequate cause for the increase. In itself, the establishment of a cause proves nothing. A bridge may have been subjected to great strain and still be unimpaired. Though at present there may be ample cause for a future rise in the securities market, some other condition may intervene and prevent its operation. The assignment of a cause can at best establish merely a *probability,* and yet the laws of cause and effect are so fundamental that man is usually loath to believe that a condition exists

The Discussion

or will exist, until he knows what has brought it
about or what will bring it about. A course of reasoning which argues that a proposition is true because the fact affirmed is the logical result of
some adequate cause is called *argument from antecedent probability*.

Simple examples of this kind of reasoning are
found in the following sentences: "It will rain because an east wind is blowing"; "As most of our
officers in the standing army have been West Point
graduates, the United States military system has
reached a high standard of efficiency." The following are more extended illustrations:—

It appears to have been fully established that, in certain
industries, various economies in production — such as
eliminating cross freights, concentrating the superintending
force, running best plants to full capacity, etc.— can be
made from production on a large scale, or, in other instances, through the combination of different establish-
ments favorably located in different sections of the country. It is, of course, not to be expected that any one
source of saving will be found applicable in all industries, nor that the importance of any will be the same
in different industries; but in many industries enough
sources of saving will be found to make combination
profitable. This statement does not ignore the fact that
there may be, in many instances, disadvantages enough to
offset the benefits; but experience does seem to show
that, in many cases, at least, the cost of manufacture and
distribution is materially lessened.

The Discussion

Granting that these savings can be made, it is evident that the influence of Industrial Combinations might readily be to lower prices to consumers.[1]

In attempting to prove that operas can be successfully produced in English, Francis Rogers says :—

We have a poetic literature of marvelous richness. Only the Germans can lay claim to a lyric wealth as great as ours. The language we inherit is an extraordinarily rich one. A German authority credits it with a vocabulary three times as large as that of France, the poorest, in number of words, of all the great languages. With such an enormous fund of words to choose from it seems as if we should be able to express our thoughts not only with unparalleled exactness and subtlety, but also with unequalled variety of sound. Further it is probable that English surpasses the other three great languages of song, German, Italian, and French, in number of distinguishable vowel sounds, but in questions of ear authorities usually differ, and it is hazardous to claim in this an indubitable supremacy. It seems certain, however, that English has rather more than twice as many vowel sounds as Italian (the poorest language in this respect), which has only seven or eight.[2]

Since reasoning from antecedent probability can at best establish only a strong presumption, and since it is often not of sufficient weight to accomplish even this, an arguer, to be successful, must

[1] Jeremiah W. Jenks, North American Review, June, 1901, page 907.

[2] Scribner's, January, 1909, p. 42.

143

know the tests that determine how strong and how weak an argument of this sort is. He may apply these tests both to his own reasoning and to the reasoning of others. The first test is :—

(1) *Is the assigned cause of sufficient strength to produce the alleged effect?*

The significance of this question is at once apparent. In the case of a criminal prosecution, it asks whether the accused had sufficient motive for performing the deed. In connection with political and economic propositions that advocate a change in existing conditions, this test asks whether the new method proposed is sufficiently virile and far-reaching actually to produce the excellent results anticipated. A few years ago the advocates of free silver were maintaining that "sixteen to one" would be a sure cure for all poverty and financial distress. A careful application of this test would have materially weakened such an argument. Believers in reformatory rather than punitive methods of imprisonment say it is antecedently probable that kind treatment, healthful surroundings, and instruction in various directions will reclaim most criminals to an honest life. Before accepting or rejecting this argument, one should decide in his own mind whether or not such treatment is adequate to make a released convict give up his former criminal practices.

If the argument stands the first test, the next question to ask is:—

(2) *May some other cause intervene and prevent the action of the assigned cause?*

During the spring of 1908 it was generally known that the Erie Railroad had no money with which to pay the interest that was about due on its outstanding bonds. Wall Street prophesied that the road would go into a receiver's hands. This result was extremely probable. Mr. Harriman, however, president of the Union Pacific, stepped in and by arranging for the payment of the interest saved the road from bankruptcy. This was an example of how an intervening cause prevented the action of the assigned cause. When Congress passed the Fifteenth Amendment to the Constitution, many people said that this legislation would inevitably cause the social, political, and financial ruin of the whole South. Since they did not take into consideration the intervening action of another cause, namely, drastic measures for negro disfranchisement by the white inhabitants of the South, their reasoning from antecedent probability was entirely erroneous.

The Discussion

2. ARGUMENT FROM SIGN.

Argument from effect to cause. The process of reasoning from effect to cause is called argument from sign. Since every circumstance must be the result of some preceding circumstance, the arguer tries to find the cause of some fact that is known to exist, and thereby to establish the existence of a hitherto unknown fact. For instance, when one sees a pond frozen over, he is likely to reason back to the cause of this condition and decide that there has been a fall in temperature, a fact that he may not have known before. The sight of smoke indicates the presence of fire. Human footprints in the snow are undoubted proof that someone has been present.

In the following quotation, the recent prohibition movement in the South is said to be a sign that the voters wish to keep liquor away from the negro:—

What is the cause of this drift toward prohibition in the South? The obvious cause, and the one most often given in explanation, is the presence of the negro. It is said that the vote for prohibition in the South represents exactly the same reasoning which excludes liquor from Indian reservations, shuts it out by international agreement from the islands of the Pacific, and excludes it from great areas in Africa under the British flag; and that,

The Discussion

wherever there is an undeveloped race, the reasons for restrictions upon the liquor traffic become convincing.[1]

The strength of this kind of reasoning depends upon the closeness of the connection between the effect and the assigned cause. In testing argument from sign, one should ask :—

(1) *Is the cause assigned adequate to produce the observed effect?*

This test is precisely the same as the test of adequacy for antecedent probability. One could not maintain that the productiveness of a certain piece of ground was due entirely to the kind of fertilizer used on it, nor that a national financial upheaval was caused by the failure of a single unimportant bank. In each of these cases the cause suggested may have assisted in producing the result, but obviously it was not of itself adequate to be the sole cause.

(2) *Could the observed effect have resulted from any other cause than the one assigned?*

If several possible causes exist, then it is necessary to consider them all, and show that all the causes except the assigned cause did not produce the observed effect. If an employer who has been robbed discovers that one of his clerks has suddenly come

[1] Atlantic Monthly, May, 1908, p. 632.

into possession of a large sum of money, he may surmise that his clerk is a thief. This argument is valueless, however, unless he can show that his employee did not receive his newly acquired wealth through inheritance, fortunate investment, or some other reasonable method. But if no other reason than burglary or embezzlement can explain the presence of this money, the argument is very strong.

One might greatly weaken the argument (quoted on page 146) which assigned the cause of the recent prohibition movement in the South to the presence of the negro by showing that this action was not the result of the assigned cause, but largely of another cause. He might prove that during the debate in the Georgia Legislature upon the pending prohibitory bill, the negro was not once mentioned as a reason for the enactment of prohibition; and that the chief arguments in favor of prohibition were based upon the fact that the saloon element had formed a political ring in the South and were controlling the election of sheriffs, mayors, aldermen, and legislators.

Argument from effect to effect. Argument from sign also includes the process of reasoning from effect to effect through a common cause. This method consists of combining the process just

The Discussion

described with the argument from antecedent probability. A reduction of wages in one cotton mill is a sign that there may be a reduction in other cotton mills. Here the reasoning goes from effect to effect, passing, however, though perhaps the reasoner is not aware that the process is so complex, through a cause common to both effects. In full, the reasoning would be: a reduction in the first mill is the result of the cause "hard times"; it is then antecedently probable that this cause will produce a similar reduction of wages in other mills.

This method may be represented by the following figure:—

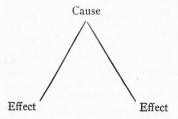

Only one effect is known; the other effect is inferred, first, by a process of reasoning from a known effect to an unknown cause, and secondly, by the process of reasoning from this assumed cause to an unknown effect.

The Discussion

This method of reasoning is sound and legitimate when both effects have the same cause. Its weakness lies in the fact that it may be attacked on two sides: on the reasoning from effect to cause, and on the reasoning from cause to effect. If the connection can be broken in either process, the argument is overthrown. The tests to be used have already been given.

3. ARGUMENT FROM EXAMPLE.

Argument from example is the name given to the process by which one reasons that what has been true under certain circumstances will again be true under the same or similar circumstances. In using this method of reasoning one argues that whenever several persons or things or conditions are alike in some respects, any given cause operating upon them will in each case produce the same effect; any line of action adopted by them will in each case have the same result.

There are two divisions of argument from example. When the resemblance between the things compared is close, the process is called argument by generalization; when the resemblance is so slight that there can be no direct comparison, but only a

The Discussion

comparison of functions, the process is called argument from analogy.

Argument by generalization. If one finds that a certain mastiff becomes with training an excellent watch dog, he may reasonably take it for granted that training will produce the same result in another dog of the same breed. If a college student with certain pronounced physical and mental characteristics is known to be an exceptionally good football player, the athletic trainer is sure to reason by generalization that another student with these same characteristics would be a valuable addition to the team. Burke in his *Speech on Conciliation* uses this kind of reasoning when he says that just as Turkey and Spain have found it necessary to govern their distant possessions with a loose rein, so,.too, England will be obliged to govern the American Colonies leniently.

Benjamin Harrison used this method of argument in the following quotation :—

That we give back to Porto Rico all the revenue derived from the customs we levy, does not seem to me to soften our dealings with her people. Our fathers were not mollified by the suggestion that the tea and stamp taxes would be expended wholly for the benefit of the colonies. It is to say: We do not need this money; it is only levied to show that your country is no part of

151

The Discussion

the United States, and that you are not citizens of the United States, save at our pleasure.[1]

Argument by generalization very rarely constitutes absolute proof. In dealing with things, it may do so in rare cases; in dealing with human actions, almost never. The reason why it can establish only a strong probability lies in a weakness in the process of reasoning.

Notice that while this kind of argument apparently reasons directly from the example cited to the case in hand, there is in reality an intermediate step. This step is a general truth of which both the known fact and the fact to be proved must be instances. When it is argued that since one mastiff makes a good watch dog another mastiff will also make a good watch dog, the reasoning passes through the general statement, "All mastiffs make good watch dogs."

Graphically the process might be represented thus :—

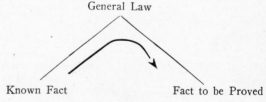

General Law

Known Fact   Fact to be Proved

[1] North American Review, January, 1901, p. 17.

The Discussion

This method is very much like the method of reasoning from effect to effect, except that here the intermediate step does not *cause,* but merely accounts for the facts. In the illustration taken from Burke, the known fact is that neither Turkey nor Spain can govern their distant provinces despotically. The general law is that no country can govern a distant dependency harshly. The fact proved is that England cannot play the despot with the American Colonies.

The weakness of this sort of reasoning is now easily seen. In the first place, there are few general laws governing human action that always hold true. In the second place, unless there is a very strong resemblance between the cases compared, unless they are alike in all essential particulars, they will not both be examples of the working of one general law.

The following quotation points out an error that might be made from too hasty reasoning by example :—

On August 23d the Southern Railway, which since 1902 had been paying 5 per cent. annual dividends on its preferred stock, voted to reduce those dividends from a 5 per cent. annual rate to one of 3. Five days later, on August 28th, the Erie Railroad, which had been paying 4 per cent. . . . announced that it would pay no

The Discussion

cash dividend this time, but would issue to the amount of the usual 4 per cent. dividend, what it called dividend warrants, which were practically notes at 4 per cent. redeemable in cash in 1907.

It was natural that this action regarding dividends should have awakened much uneasiness. . . . To predict a similar cutting of dividends by other railway companies would, however, be unwarranted. The case of the Southern Railway and the Erie was peculiar. Each had been classed among the financially weak railways of the country. Both were reorganized from absolute railway wrecks, and in each the new scheme of capitalization was proposed to the markets at a time when recovery from the depression of 1893 had not made such progress as it had achieved when the greater companies, like the Union Pacific, were reorganized. The result was that, with both these railways, provisions of working capital and adjustment of liabilities to the possible needs of an active industrial future were inadequately made.[1]

An excellent illustration of how to refute argument by generalization is found in the following quotation. It has been said that since England finds free trade beneficial, the United States should adopt the same policy. Mr. Reed, a leading advocate of protection, points out the weakness of this argument.

According to the usual story that is told, England had been engaged with a long and vain struggle with the demon of protection, and had been year after year sinking farther into the depths, until at a moment when she

[1] Alexander D. Noyes, The Forum, October-December, 1907, p. 198.

The Discussion

was in her distress and saddest plight, her manufacturing system broke down, "protection, having destroyed home trade by reducing," as Mr. Atkinson says, "the entire population to beggary, destitution, and want." Mr. Cobden and his friends providentially appeared, and after a hard struggle established a principle for all time and for all the world, and straightway England enjoyed the sum of human happiness. Hence all good nations should do as England has done and be happy ever after.

Suppose England, instead of being a little island in the sea, had been the half of a great continent full of raw material, capable of an internal commerce which would rival the commerce of all the rest of the world.

Suppose every year new millions were flocking to her shores, and every one of those new millions in a few years, as soon as they tasted the delights of a broader life, would become as great a consumer as any one of her own people.

Suppose that these millions, and the 70,000,000 already gathered under the folds of her flag, were every year demanding and receiving a higher wage and therefore broadening her market as fast as her machinery could furnish production. Suppose she had produced cheap food beyond all her wants, and that her laborers spent so much money that whether wheat was sixty cents a bushel or twice that sum hardly entered the thoughts of one of them except when some democratic tariff bill was paralyzing his business.

Suppose that she was not only but a cannon shot from France, but that every country in Europe had been brought as near to her as Baltimore is to Washington — for that is what cheap ocean freights mean between us and European producers. Suppose all those countries had her machinery, her skilled workmen, her industrial system, and labor forty per cent. cheaper. Suppose under that state of facts, with all her manufactures proclaiming against it, frantic in their disapproval, England had been called upon by Cobden to make the plunge into free trade, would she have done it? Not if Cobden had been backed by the angelic host. History gives England credit for great sense.[1]

Argument from analogy. When two instances of objects which are *unlike in themselves,* but which *perform similar functions or have similar relations,* are compared for the sake of showing that what is true in one case is true in the other, the process is called *argument from analogy.* The following quotation is a good illustration of this kind of argument:—

" Mr. Pinchot compared our present consumption of wood to the case of a man in an open boat at sea, cut adrift from some shipwreck and with but a few days' supply of water on board. He drinks all the water the first day, simply because he is thirsty, though he knows that the water will not last long. The American people know that their wood supply will last but a few decades. Yet they shut their eyes to the facts."

Water and wood are not alike in themselves; they cannot be directly compared, but they are alike in the relations they bear to other circumstances.

When President Lincoln refused to change generals at a certain time during the Civil War, saying

[1] Thomas B. Reed, Speech in House of Representatives, Feb. 1, 1904.

that it was not wise to " swap horses while crossing a stream," he reasoned from analogy. Since the horse in taking its master across the stream and the general in conducting a campaign are totally unlike in themselves but have similar relations, the argument is from analogy and not from generalization.

It is easy to see that such reasoning never constitutes indubitable proof. If argument from generalization, where the objects compared differ from each other in only a few respects, is weak, plainly, argument from analogy is much weaker, since the objects are alike merely in the relations they bear.

Though argument from analogy does not constitute proof, yet it is often valuable as a means of illustration. Truths frequently need illumination more than verification, and in such cases this sort of comparison may be very useful. Many proverbs are condensed arguments from analogy, their strength depending upon the similarity between the known case and the case in hand. It is not hard to find the analogy in these expressions : " Lightning never strikes twice in the same place "; " Don't count your chickens before they are hatched "; " A fool and his money are soon parted."

The student who has carefully read this chapter

The Discussion

up to this point should have a fairly clear idea of the nature of proof; he should know that proof consists of evidence and reasoning; he should know the tests for each of these; and he should be able to distinguish between strong and weak arguments. The next step for him to take will be to apply these instructions in generating proof for any statement that he wishes to establish.

A common fault in argumentation is the failure to support important points with sufficient proof. One or two points well established will go farther toward inducing belief in a proposition than a dozen points that are but weakly substantiated. A statement should be proved not only by inductive reasoning, but, if possible, by deductive. If one uses argument from antecedent probability in establishing a statement, he should not rest content with this one method of proof, but he should try also to use argument from sign, and argument from example, and, whenever he can, he should quote authority.

Notice that in the following outline three kinds of proof are used. The amount of proof here given is by no means sufficient to establish the truth of the proposition being upheld; the outline, however,

The Discussion

does illustrate the proper method of building up the proof of a proposition.

The present condition of the United States Senate is deplorable.

Antecedent Probability.

I. The present method of electing Senators is ample cause for such a condition, since

    A. Senators are not responsible to any one, as

        1. They are not responsible to the people, for

           a. The people do not elect them.

        2. They are not responsible to the legislature, for

           a. The legislature changes inside of six years.

Sign.

II. There is ample evidence to prove that the condition is deplorable.

    A. States are often unrepresented in the Senate. (Haynes' *Election of Senators,* page 158.)

    B. Many Senators have fallen into disrepute, for

The Discussion

1. One out of every ten members of the Fifty-eighth Congress had been before the courts on criminal charges. (Harper's Weekly, Vol. XLIV, page 113.)

C. Many Senators have engaged in fist fights on the floor of the Senate Chamber.

Authority.

III. Prominent men testify to its deplorable condition. (A. M. Low, North American Review, Vol. CLXXIV, page 231; D. G. Phillips, Cosmopolitan, Vol. XL, page 487.)

PERSUASION.

Though it has been stated in a previous chapter that the persuasive portions of an argument should be found for the most part in the introduction and the conclusion, still persuasion in the discussion is extremely important. It is true that the real work of the discussion is to prove the proposition; but if conviction alone be used, there is great danger, in most cases, that the arguer will weary his audience, lose their attention, and thus fail to drive home the ideas that he wishes them to adopt. Since

The Discussion

everything depends upon how the arguer has already treated his subject, and how it has been received by the audience, specific directions for persuasion in the discussion cannot possibly be given. Suggestions in regard to this matter must be even more abstract and general than were the directions for persuasion in the introduction.

To begin with, persuasion in the discussion should usually be of a supplementary nature. Unless the arguer has won the attention and, to some extent at least, the good will of his audience before he commences upon his proof, he may as well confess failure and proceed no farther. If, however, the persuasiveness of his introduction has accomplished the purpose for which it exists, he may introduce his proof without hesitation, taking care all the time to interweave enough persuasion to maintain the favorable impression that he has already made.

In general, the directions for doing this are the same as those for securing persuasion in the introduction. In both divisions *modesty, fairness,* and *sincerity,* are the characteristics that make for success. The same conditions that demand these qualities in one place require their use throughout the whole argument. Then, too, it is often effective to make occasionally an appeal to some strong emotion. As a rule, the attitude of the modern audience is essentially one of indifference, of so great indifference that special effort must be made first to gain, then to hold, their attention. The direct emotional appeal, when the subject, the occasion, and the audience are such that there is no danger of its being ludicrous, will usually accomplish this result. If such a method, however, is manifestly out of place, other means must be sought for producing a similar effect.

One of the very commonest devices for gaining attention is to relate a short anecdote. Everybody enjoys a good story, and if it is chosen with proper regard for its illustrative value, the argument is sure to be strengthened. On the whole, humorous stories are best. They often relieve the tedium of an otherwise dry speech, and not only serve as persuasion, but drive home a point with greater emphasis than could the most elaborate course of reasoning. This method is so familiar to every one that detailed explanation is unnecessary. Owing to the limited amount of time at their command, student debaters can, as a rule, use only the very shortest stories, and these should be chosen for their illustrative rather than for their persuasive value;

The Discussion

in written arguments greater latitude is possible.

Another method that often finds favor in both written and spoken arguments is the introduction of a paragraph showing the importance of the topic under consideration. Oftentimes the arguer can show that this particular phase of the subject is of wider significance than at first appears. Perhaps he can draw a picture that will turn a seemingly uninteresting and commonplace subject into one that is teeming with romance and wonderment. For example, consider the following extract from Burke's speech on *Conciliation with the American Colonies* :—

This is the relative proportion of the importance of the colonies at these two periods : and all reasoning concerning our mode of treating them must have this proportion as its basis; or it is a reasoning weak, rotten and sophistical.

Mr. Speaker, I cannot prevail on myself to hurry over this great consideration. It is good for us to be here. We stand where we have an immense view of what is, and what is passed. Clouds, indeed, and darkness rest upon the future. Let us, however, before we descend from this noble eminence, reflect that this growth of our national prosperity has happened within the short period of the life of man. It has happened within sixty-eight years. There are those alive whose memory might touch the two extremities. For instance, my Lord Bathurst might remember all the stages of the progress. He was in 1704 of an age at least to be made to comprehend such things. He was then old enough *acta parentum jam*

The Discussion

legere, et quae sit poterit cognoscere virtus. Suppose, sir, that the angel of this auspicious youth, foreseeing the many virtues which made him one of the most amiable, as he is one of the most fortunate, men of his age, had opened to him in vision, that when in the fourth generation the third prince of the House of Brunswick had sat twelve years on the throne of that nation which (by the happy issue of moderate and healing counsels) was to be made Great Britain, he should see his son, Lord Chancellor of England, turn back the current of hereditary dignity to its fountain and raise him to an higher rank of peerage, whilst he enriched the family with a new one;—if, amidst these bright and happy scenes of domestic honor and prosperity, that angel should have drawn up the curtain and unfolded the rising glories of his country, and, whilst he was gazing with admiration on the then commercial grandeur of England, the genius should point out to him a little speck, scarcely visible in the mass of the national interests, a small seminal principle rather than a formed body, and should tell him,— "Young man, there is America, which at this day serves for little more than to amuse you with stories of savage men and uncouth manners; yet shall, before you taste of death, show itself equal to the whole of that commerce which now attracts the envy of the world. Whatever England has been growing to by a progressive increase of improvement, brought in by varieties of people, by succession of civilizing conquests and civilizing settlements in a series of seventeen hundred years, you shall see as much added to her by America in the course of a single life!" If this state of his country had been foretold to him, would it not require all the sanguine credulity of youth and all the fervid glow of enthusiasm to make him believe it? Fortunate man, he has lived to see it! Fortunate indeed, if he lives to see nothing that shall

The Discussion

vary the prospect and cloud the setting of his day!
Excuse me, sir, if, turning from such thoughts, I re-
sume this comparative view once more.[1]

These devices an arguer will often find helpful
for bringing an element of persuasion into his proof,
but he should aim at a type of persuasion much
more effective, yet much harder to attain, than is
the result of any mere device. Proof is the strongest when each separate bit of it appeals both to
the reason and the emotions. If an arguer can
connect his subject with the feelings of his audience
and then introduce reasoning processes that will at
the same time both convince them and play upon
their feelings, he is certain to attain a large measure
of success. Although not all subjects readily lend
themselves to this method of treatment, yet if the
debater will go to the very bottom of his subject
and consider the real significance of the question
he is arguing upon, he can usually succeed in making his conviction persuasive and his persuasion
convincing. Undoubtedly the best way for a student to train himself in this respect is to study great
arguments. The following quotation from Beecher's speech in Liverpool, delivered before an audi-

[1] Speech in House of Commons, March 22, 1775.

ence composed mostly of men engaged in manufacturing, is an excellent example of persuasive proof :—

The things required for prosperous labor, prosperous manufactures, and prosperous commerce are three : first, liberty; secondly, liberty; thirdly, liberty — but these are not merely the same liberty, as I shall show you.

First, there must be liberty to follow those laws of business which experience has developed, without imposts or restrictions, or governmental intrusions. Business simply wants to be let alone.

Then, secondly, there must be liberty to distribute and exchange products of industry in any market without burdensome tariffs, without imposts, and without vexatious regulations. There must be these two liberties — liberty to create wealth, as the makers of it think best according to the light and experience which business has given them; and then liberty to distribute what they have created without unnecessary vexatious burdens. The comprehensive law of the ideal industrial condition of the world is free manufacture and free trade.

I have said there were three elements of liberty. The third is the necessity of an intelligent and free race of customers. There must be freedom among producers; there must be freedom among the distributors; there must be freedom among the customers. It may not have occurred to you that it makes any difference what one's customers are; but it does, in all regular and prolonged business. The condition of the customer determines how much he will buy, determines of what sort he will buy. Poor and ignorant people buy little and that of the poorest kind. The richest and the intelligent, having the more means to buy, buy the most, and always buy the best.

Here, then, are the three liberties: liberty of the pro-

The Discussion

ducer, liberty of the distributor, and liberty of the consumer. The first two need no discussion — they have been
long, thoroughly, and brilliantly illustrated by the political
economists of Great Britain, and by her eminent statesmen; but it seems to me that enough attention has not
been directed to the third, and, with your patience, I will
dwell on that for a moment, before proceeding to other
topics.

It is a necessity of every manufacturing and commercial
people that their customers should be very wealthy and
intelligent. Let us put the subject before you in the familiar light of your own local experience. To whom do
the tradesmen of Liverpool sell the most goods at the
highest profit? To the ignorant and poor, or to the educated and prosperous? The poor man buys simply for his
body; he buys food, he buys clothing, he buys fuel, he
buys lodging. His rule is to buy the least and the cheap-
est that he can. He goes to the store as seldom as he
can,— he brings away as little as he can — and he buys
for the least he can. Poverty is not a misfortune to the
poor only who suffer it, but it is more or less a misfortune to all with whom they deal.

On the other hand, a man well off — how is it with
him? He buys in far greater quantity. He can afford to
do it; he has the money to pay for it. He buys in far
greater variety, because he seeks to gratify not merely
physical wants, but also mental wants. He buys for the
satisfaction of sentiment and taste, as well as of sense.
He buys silk, wool, flax, cotton; he buys all metals —
iron, silver, gold, platinum; in short, he buys for all
necessities and of all substances. But that is not all. He
buys a better quality of goods. He buys richer silks,
finer cottons, higher grained wools. Now, a rich silk
means so much skill and care of somebody's that has
been expended upon it to make it finer and richer; and
so of cotton, and so of wool. That is, the price of the

167

The Discussion

finer goods runs back to the very beginning, and remunerates the workman as well as the merchant. Indeed, the whole laboring community is as much interested and profited as the mere merchant, in this buying and selling of the higher grades in the greater varieties and quantities.

The law of price is the skill; and the amount of skill expended in the work is as much for the market as are the goods. A man comes to the market and says, " I have a pair of hands "; and he obtains the lowest wages. Another man comes and says, " I have something more than a pair of hands — I have truth and fidelity "; he gets a higher price. Another man comes and says, " I have something more; I have hands and strength, and fidelity, and skill." He gets more than either of the others. The next man comes and says, " I have got hands and strength, and skill, and fidelity; but my hands work more than that. They know how to create things for the fancy, for the affections, for the moral sentiments "; and he gets more than any of the others. The last man comes and says, " I have all these qualities, and have them so highly that it is a peculiar genius "; and genius carries the whole market and gets the highest price. So that both the workman and the merchant are profited by having purchasers that demand quality, variety, and quantity.

Now, if this be so in the town or the city, it can only be so because it is a law. This is the specific development of a general or universal law, and therefore we should expect to find it as true of a nation as of a city like Liverpool. I know it is so, and you know that it is true of all the world; and it is just as important to have customers educated, intelligent, moral, and rich, out of Liverpool as it is in Liverpool. They are able to buy; they want variety; they want the very best; and those are the customers you want. That nation is the best customer

168

The Discussion

that is freest, because freedom works prosperity, industry, and wealth. Great Britain, then, aside from moral considerations, has a direct commercial and pecuniary interest in the liberty, civilization, and wealth of every people and every nation on the globe.

You have also an interest in this, because you are a moral and a religious people. You desire it from the highest motives, and godliness is profitable in all things, having the promise of the life that is, as well as of that which is to come; but if there were no hereafter, and if man had no progress in this life, and if there were no question of moral growth at all, it would be worth your while to protect civilization and liberty, merely as a commercial speculation. To evangelize has more than a moral and religious import — it comes back to temporal relations. Wherever a nation that is crushed, cramped, degraded under despotism, is struggling to be free, you, Leeds, Sheffield, Manchester, Paisley, all have an interest that that nation should be free. When depressed and backward people demand that they may have a chance to rise — Hungary, Italy, Poland — it is a duty for humanity's sake, it is a duty for the highest moral motives, to sympathize with them; but beside all these there is a material and an interested reason why you should sympathize with them. Pounds and pence join with conscience and with honor in this design.[1]

EXERCISES

A. In the following passage point out all assertions that are made, note whether the source of the evidence is definitely stated, and test the witnesses that give the evidence.

Reciprocity is the only remedy for the commercial an-

[1] The World's Famous Orations, Vol. X, p. 12. Funk and Wagnalls Company.

The Discussion

tagonism which is fast separating Canada and the United States. Canada has long waited in vain for the culmination of treaties whereby she can trade with us on equal terms. Now, angered by our long evasion of the question, she is, according to prominent Canadian statesmen, contemplating the passage of high protective tariff laws, which will effectually close the doors of Canadian trade to us. Canada is young, but she is growing fast. The value of her imports is steadily growing larger, and if we do not make some concession to her we shall lose this vast trade. She makes and sells many things of which we do not have a home supply. Why not then open our doors to her and admit her products? Would it not be of distinct advantage to us?

The American Press is almost unanimous in declaring that the sum of the advantages attending this step would far offset any disadvantages. For instance, the supply of lumber in the United States is fast becoming exhausted; experts say that in fifteen years we shall have a lumber famine. If we turn to Canada, however, we see her mountain slopes green with trees and her wooded valleys covered with millions of feet of lumber. Why, then, not get our lumber from Canada and preserve what few forests we do have? Because of the exorbitant tariff on imported lumber. Lumber at its present high prices is even cheap compared with the price of imported lumber. Moreover, lumber is not the only article that is expensive here, though it is cheap just across the line in Canada. The World's Work, Vol. V, page 2979, says that reciprocity with Canada would cheapen many articles that are now costly.

B. Point out the kind of reasoning found in each of the following arguments:—

1. The wholesale destruction of the forests in many States portends the loss of our whole timber supply.

The Discussion

2. His faithful performance of every duty assures him an early promotion.

3. Since he succeeded well in his college work, it is an assured fact that he will make a brilliant reputation for himself in business.

4. Cæsar had his Brutus, Charles I his Cromwell, and George III — may profit by their example.

5. The well-tilled fields, the carefully-trimmed hedges, and the sleek appearance of the stock bespoke a thrifty and industrious farmer.

6. You tried in Wales to raise a revenue which the people thought excessive and unjust: the attempt ended in oppression, resistance, rebellion, and loss to yourselves. You tried in the Duchy of Lancaster to raise a revenue which the people believed unjust: this effort ended in oppression, rebellion, vexation, and loss to yourselves. You are now trying to raise in America a revenue which the Colonists disapprove. What must be the result?

7. Then, sir, from these six capital sources: of descent; of form of government; of religion in the northern provinces; of manners in the southern; of education; of the remoteness of situation from the first mover of government — from all these causes a fierce spirit of liberty has grown up.

8. Collective bargaining is an advantage to working men; it tends to give them some share in the control of the industry to which they contribute.

9. That a free labor union is not the impractical dream of an idealist is to be found in the fact that some of the greatest and most successful of the labor organizations have always adhered to the principle of the open shop. In the Pennsylvania coal-mines union and non-union miners labored together in the same mine and reaped the same benefits from the collective bargaining carried on for them by John Mitchell. In the recent

The Discussion

anarchy in Colorado, the one mine which went on with its work peacefully, prosperously, and without disturbance, until it was closed by military orders, was a mine which maintained the principle of the open shop, and in which union and non-union men worked peacefully together.

10. Suppose that all the property you were worth was in gold, and you had put it in the hands of Blondin, the famous rope-walker, to carry across the Niagara Falls on a tight rope. Would you shake the rope while he was passing over it, or keep shouting to him, " Blondin, stoop a little more! Go a little faster!" No, I am sure you would not. You would hold your breath as well as your tongue, and keep your hand off until he was safely over. Now the government is in the same situation. It is carrying an immense weight across a stormy ocean. Untold treasures are in its hands. It is doing the best it can. Don't badger it! Just keep still and it will get you safely over.

C. Prove or disprove the following statements, using, wherever it is possible, argument from antecedent probability, sign, example, and authority. Give references for all evidence except generally admitted facts.

1. The negro is not prepared to receive the same kind of education that the white man receives.

2. Railway pooling lowers freight rates.

3. The election of Senators by State Legislatures is undemocratic.

4. The present commercial relations between Canada and the United States are detrimental to the industries of the United States.

5. The influence of labor unions has greatly diminished child labor in the United States.

6. Woman suffrage would purify politics.

7. Egypt is benefited by the control of England.

8. Strikes benefit the working man.

172

The Discussion

9. The municipal ownership of street railways is a financial failure.

10. Lumber companies threaten the extermination of the forests in the United States.

CHAPTER VII

THE DISCUSSION — BRIEF-DRAWING

The second division of a brief, corresponding to the second division of a complete argument, is called the *discussion*. In this part of his brief the arguer logically arranges all the evidence and reasoning that he wishes to use in establishing or overthrowing his proposition. Illustrative material, rhetorical embellishment, and other forms of persuasion that may enter into the finished argument are omitted, but the real proof is complete in the brief.

There are two possible systems of arranging proof. For the sake of convenience they may be called the " because " method and the " therefore " method. These methods derive their names from the connectives that are used. When the " because " method is used, the proof follows the statement being established, and is connected to this statement with some such word as: *as, because, for,* or *since.* To illustrate :—

Brief of the Discussion

I. Expenses at a country college are less than at a city college, *because*

    A. At the country college room rent is cheaper.

    B. Table board costs less.

    C. Amusement places are less numerous.

Under the "therefore" method, the proof precedes the statement being established; the connectives are *hence* and *therefore*. The previous argument arranged in this form would read as follows:—

    A. Since room rent is cheaper at the country college than at the city college, and

    B. Since table board costs less, and

    C. Since amusement places are less numerous, *therefore*.

      I. Expenses at a country college are less than at a city college.

The student should always use the "because" method of arrangement. It is preferable to the "therefore" method since it affords a much easier apprehension of the argument advanced. If the reader of the brief has the conclusion in his mind at the very start, he can test the strength and adequacy of the proof very quickly, and can, perhaps, the first time he reads the argument form an opinion as to its worth. But he will almost always have difficulty in grasping the significance of evidence and reasoning before he knows what the proof is expected to prove. The "therefore" method usually obliges a careful reasoner, after finally reaching the conclusion, to go over the whole proof a second time.

To assist the student in carrying out the proper arrangement of his proof, two rules have been formulated. One rule deals with main headings, the headings marked with the Roman numerals; the other deals with subordinate headings.

Rule IX. *Phrase each principal statement in the discussion so that it will read as a reason for the truth or the falsity of the proposition.*

Rule X. *Phrase each subordinate statement in the discussion so that it will read as a reason for the truth of the statement to which it is subordinate. The connectives to be used are: as, because, for, and since.*

In connection with the first of these rules, notice that principal headings read as reasons for the truth or the falsity of the proposition. Obviously they read as reasons for the truth if the brief is on the affirmative side, and for the falsity if the brief is on the negative side. Headings and subheadings should always be supported, not demolished.

The error of making unsupported statements in a complete argument has already been discussed. Assertion in a brief is equally faulty. To insure belief, all statements must rest ultimately either upon the testimony of witnesses or upon statements admitted to be true.

Notice how unconvincing is the following portion of a brief:—

Proposition — American cities should own and operate all street-car lines within their limits.

I. The present system of operating street-car lines is efficient, for

    A. The street-car service in the United States is the best in the world.

    B. Street-car fare in the United States is remarkably low.

The insertion of testimony, however, to substantiate A and B turns this bit of brief into excellent proof.

I. The present system of operating street-car lines is efficient, for

    A. The street-car service in the United States is the best in the world, because

        1. It is best in respect to extent, since

            a. James W. Garner says that England has less than a quarter of the street-car facilities found in the United States. (Dial, Feb. 1908, p. 20.)

b. In 1902, two hundred and ninety-five communities in the United Kingdom of from 8,000 to 25,-000 inhabitants were without street cars; while in the United States there were only twenty-one such communities. (Municipal and Private Operation of Public Utilities, W. J. Clark, Vol. I, p. 445.)

2. It is best in regard to equipment and accommodation, since

a. The cars are the best equipped in the world. (Ibid.)

b. The cars are run with shorter intervals between them than anywhere else in the world. (Ibid.)

B. The fare in the United States is remarkably low, because

1. Although the fare in Glasgow, a leading exponent of municipal ownership, is but twopence, yet it will

carry one only eight miles; but five
cents in New York will carry one
fifty miles.

Rule XI. *Make no unsupported statements unless
they are generally admitted to be true.*

It has already been shown that the arguer must
reveal to his audience the sources from which he
gathered his evidence. If he gained certain information from magazines, he should state definitely
the name, the volume, and the page; if he gained
his information elsewhere, he should be equally
explicit. Since this knowledge of the source of
the evidence is essential to the success of the proof,
a statement of the sources is a part of the work of
conviction. Accordingly, these sources must be
stated in the brief as well as in the expanded argument. Thus the rule:—

Rule XII. *After all evidence state in parentheses
the source from which it came.*

In addition to establishing the side of the proposition which it advocates, a good brief almost invariably refutes the main arguments of the opposite side. The way in which this refutation is
expressed is very important. A brief on the affirmative side of the proposition, " *Resolved,* That
the Panama canal should be built at sea-level,"

would be weak and ludicrous, if, when answering the argument for the negative that the cost of a sea-level canal would be enormous, it should contain the following reasoning:—

The Panama Canal should be built at sea-level. (for)

    I.   The cost would not be much greater than for a lock canal.

One might think from this statement that the drawer of the brief considered the contention that the sea-level type would cost a little though not much more than the other type, a positive argument in favor of the sea-level canal. In reality it is nothing of the sort. The arguer is merely trying to destroy his opponent's argument to the effect that expense is an obstacle in the way of the sea-level type. This refutation should be expressed in such a manner as to show that it is refutation and not positive proof. It might well read something like this:—

The Panama Canal should be built at sea-level. (for)

    I.   The contention of the negative that a sea-level canal would cost enormously more than a lock-canal is unsound, since,

        A.   Etc.

Brief of the Discussion

Notice that this form of refutation states clearly the argument to be answered. No doubt can arise from such a statement as to the direction the argument is taking; no confusion can occur between refutation and positive proof. Hence the rule:—

Rule XIII. *Phrase refutation so that the argument to be answered is clearly stated.*

THE CONCLUSION.

As there is but one rule for brief-drawing that applies to the conclusion, it may well be given at this point. The purpose and the value of this rule are so apparent that no explanation is necessary.

Rule XIV. *Put into the conclusion a summary of the essential points established in the discussion.*

RULES FOR BRIEF-DRAWING.

General Rules.

I. *Divide the brief into three parts, and mark them respectively, Introduction, Discussion, and Conclusion.*

II. *Express each idea in the brief in the form of a complete statement.*

Brief of the Discussion

III. *Make in each statement only a single assertion.*

IV. *Make each statement as concise as is consistent with clearness.*

V. *Indicate the relation between statements by indentation and by the use of symbols.*

VI. *Mark each statement with only one symbol.*

Rules for the Introduction.

VII. *Put into the introduction sufficient explanation for a complete understanding of the discussion. This explanation usually involves (a) a definition of terms, (b) an explanation of the meaning of the proposition, (c) a statement of the issues, and (d) the partition.*

VIII. *Put into the introduction only statements admitted by both sides.*

Rules for the · Discussion.

IX. *Phrase each principal statement in the discussion so that it will read as a reason for the truth or the falsity of the proposition.*

X. *Phrase each subordinate statement in the discussion so that it will read as a reason for the truth of the statement to which it is subordinate. The*

Brief of the Discussion

connectives to be used are: as, because, for, and since.

XI. *Make no unsupported statements unless they are generally admitted to be true.*

XII. *After all evidence state in parentheses the source from which it came.*

XIII. *Phrase refutation so that the argument to be answered is clearly stated.*

Rule for the Conclusion.

XIV. *Put into the conclusion a summary of the essential points established in the discussion.*

MODEL BRIEF.

Resolved, That immigration to the United States should be further restricted by an educational test.

Affirmative Brief.

INTRODUCTION.

I.   The question of further restricting immigration to the United States by an educational test gains in importance from the alleged impairment of American institutions and standards by immigration.

Brief of the Discussion

II. The following explanations will aid in the discussion of the question:—

   A. Immigration to the United States means the migrating of people into the United States for the purpose of permanent residence. (Century Dictionary.)

   B. The restrictive measures now in force are as follows:—

      1. Idiots, insane persons, paupers, convicts, diseased persons, anarchists, polygamists, women for immoral purposes, assisted aliens, contract laborers, and the Chinese are excluded. (Statutes of the United States.)

      2. A head tax of four dollars is imposed. (Ibid.)

   C. The proposed restrictive measure is as follows:—

      1. Every immigrant to the United States between the ages of fifteen and fifty must be able to read and write a few sentences of some language. (Congressional Record, Vol. XXVIII, page 5421.)

Brief of the Discussion

III. The points to be determined seem to be :—

    A. Is there a need for further restriction of immigration?

    B. If there is such a need, would the educational test accomplish this further restriction in a proper manner?

DISCUSSION.

I. There is great need for further restriction of immigration, because

    A. The character of the immigrants since 1880 has greatly changed for the worse, for

        1. Before 1880 most of the immigrants were earnest, energetic people from northern and western Europe. (International Encyclopædia, under Immigration.)

        2. At the present time seventy and one-half per cent. of the total number of immigrants are from the unenergetic people of southern and eastern Europe. (Ibid.)

        3. More immigrants have become paupers than was formerly the case, for

Brief of the Discussion

    a. Prior to 1880 there were comparatively few paupers among the immigrants. (Ibid.)

    b. At present the percentage of pauperism among the foreigners here is four times as great as among the natives. (Ibid.)

4. While the Germans, English, and other immigrants from northern Europe who came here before 1880 were moral and upright, the present immigrants from southern Europe have a low code of morals, for

    a. The moral degeneracy of the races of southern Europe is well known. (Henry Rood, Forum, Vol. XIV, page 116.)

5. Crime among foreigners in this country has increased immensely, for

    a. In 1905 twenty-eight per cent. of our criminals were of foreign birth. (Report of the Commissioner-General of Immigration for 1905.)

6. Illiteracy among immigrants has greatly increased, for

Brief of the Discussion

        a. In 1905 the percentage of illiter-
            ates of foreign birth was twen-
            ty-six. (Ibid.)
        b. Many of the present immigrants
            are illiterates from southern
            Italy. (S. E. Moffett, Review
            of Reviews, Vol. 28, page 55.)
B. The condition of the cities and especially
    of their slum districts is alarming, for
    1. The number of immigrants is increas-
        ing astonishingly, inasmuch as,
        a. 8,385 immigrants arrived in 1820.
        b. 788,992 immigrants arrived in
            1882.
        c. 1,026,499 immigrants arrived in
            1905. (Report of Commis-
            sioner-General of Immigration,
            1905, page 42.)
    2. Two-thirds of the total number of im-
        migrants in 1902 settled in the
        cities. (Editorial in Outlook, Vol.
        LXXI, page 154.)
    3. These congested districts foster un-
        sanitary conditions, physical degen-
        eration, and crime. (Deputy Clerk
        of Children's Court, New York

City, North American Review, Vol.
CLXXIX, page 731.)

4. Charitable organizations are unable to
cope with the problems in congested
districts, for

   a. The number of immigrants is increasing too rapidly. (Report
of Commissioner-General of
Immigration, 1905.)

C. The present immigration is politically
harmful, for

  1. Immigrants of the kind that are now
coming in do not make good citizens, because

   a. They are indifferent to civic manners, for

     1'. They cannot appreciate the
spirit of American government, as has previously
been shown.

   b. They are easily influenced in all
political affairs by pecuniary
persuasion, for

     1'. Their sole object in this coun-
try is to acquire wealth.
(Prescott F. Hall, Secretary

Brief of the Discussion

of the Immigration Restriction League, Annals of American Academy, Vol. XXIV, page 172.)

D. The number of immigrants is too great to be assimilated properly, since

   1. Most of the immigrants are extremely clannish, for

      a. "Little Italies," "Little Hungaries," and "Ghettos," exist in great numbers and size throughout the United States. (Henry Rood, Forum, Vol. XIV, page 114.)

   2. Most of the immigrants never try to learn the English language, for

      a. They have no need for it, since

         1′. They seldom come in contact with English-speaking people. (Ibid.)

   3. Their tendency is not to become citizens, for

      a. Thirty-one per cent. of the immigrants return home after having been here a few years. (Report of the Commissioner-

189

Brief of the Discussion

General of Immigration, 1905.)

b. Those who remain cannot for the most part appreciate our government, for

1′. They have been continually trodden upon in their home countries.

2′. They have had no opportunity to interest themselves in government. (N. S. Shaler, Atlantic Monthly, Vol. LXXI, page 646.)

4. The argument that because we were able to assimilate the immigrants in the past we shall be able to do so in the future, is unsound, for

a. The character of the present immigrants has changed, as shown previously.

b. In the future we may expect a much larger immigration. (Prescott F. Hall, Annals of American Academy, Vol. XXIV, page 172.)

E. Immigrants lower the standards of American labor, because

Brief of the Discussion

1. They create harmful competition, since
   a. More immigrants are coming now than we really need, for
      1'. In 1906 at least 200,000 aliens came here who were of no use whatever. (Commissioner of Immigration for New York, Popular Science Monthly, Vol. LXVI, page 175.)
   b. They work for lower wages than do Americans, for
      1'. They are able to live more cheaply. (Henry Rood, Ibid.)
      2'. They place a lower value on their labor. (T. V. Powderly, North American Review, Vol. CXLVII, page 165.)
2. They tend to destroy the independence of the American laborer, for
   a. They work under conditions that no American laborer will tolerate, for
      1'. They create degrading forms

of employment. (W. H. Wilkins, Nineteenth Century, Vol. XXX, page 588.)

b. Their selfish desires keep them from organizing with American laborers for protection.

II. The educational test would accomplish the further restriction of immigration in a proper manner, for

A. It would change the character of the immigrants for the better, since

1. It would keep out the unenergetic races of southern and eastern Europe, because

a. Ninety-three per cent. of illiterates come from southern and eastern Europe. (International Encyclopædia, under Immigration.)

2. It would decrease the amount of pauperism, for

a. The southern Italians, who are the most illiterate, produce the most pauperism. (Ibid.)

3. It would raise the standard of morality, since

Brief of the Discussion

    a. Ignorance is closely coupled with immorality, for

        1'. The southern Italians have a very low standard of living in the United States. (Henry Rood, Forum, Vol. XIV, page 116.)

    b. The educational test would exclude such people.

4. It would decrease the amount of crime, for

    a. It would keep out most of the immigrants from southern Europe, for

        1'. Ninety-three per cent. of the illiterates come from this source.

    b. The criminal tendencies of people from southern Europe are well known. (Henry Rood, Ibid.)

B. The educational test would improve the condition of the cities, for

1. They would be more sanitary and less criminal, since

    a. These evils are due largely to congestion.

Brief of the Discussion

      b.   Under this test the cities would be less congested, for

           1′. Immigration would be reduced twenty-two and six tenths per cent.

           2′. Educated immigrants are not likely to settle in the slums.

      c.   If the cities were less congested, charitable societies could remove more evils from the slums, and in time even eliminate the slums.

C. The educational test would aid the country politically, for

    1. We should receive only those immigrants who are intellectually capable of becoming good citizens, for

      a.   Education enables a man to become interested in the government in which he lives.

    2. Bribery would cease, for

      a.   Greed for small amounts of money is not so strong among the intelligent. (Prescott F. Hall, Ibid.)

Brief of the Discussion

D. The educational test would aid the work of assimilation, for

1. It would bar to a great extent the clannish immigrants, as

   a. Clannishness is largely a result of superstition and i g n o r a n c e. (Henry Rood, Ibid.)

2. It would practically force the immigrants to learn the English language, for

   a. Their clans broken up, they would naturally come in contact more and more with English-speaking people.

3. It would produce among the foreign-born element of the United States a wider interest in civic affairs, for

   a. Those who have some education can better appreciate our government than those who are illiterate.

   b. It would admit only those who, by reason of their education, small though it may be, have had the chance to study somewhat their

Brief of the Discussion

home governments. (N. S. Shaler, Ibid.)

E. The educational test would tend to raise the standards of American labor, for

1. It would cut down competition, since

    a. It would shut out many laborers, for

    1'. Most of those affected by this test would be common laborers.

    b. It would tend to equalize the rate of wages, because

    1'. Immigrants would not be willing to work for lower wages, for

    a'. The slums being gone, they would need more money for existence.

2. It would aid the independence of American labor, for

    a. Immigrants would no longer be so reluctant to co-operate with American laborers for protection, for

    1'. It is well known that, as a rule, only the most ignorant

196

classes refuse to join
unions.

b. The low industrial competition
would be removed, as previously
shown.

F. The educational test would be practical,
for

1. It is not a test depending upon the
representations of immigrants or the
decisions of inspectors. (Prescott
F. Hall, Forum, Vol. XXX, page
564.)

2. The educational test has worked well
in Australia. (Professor F r a n k
Parsons, Annals of American Academy, Vol. XXIV, page 215.)

G. It would lessen the burden of education
for the government, for

1. It would force prospective immigrants
to get their elementary education in
Europe.

2. The immigrants would have some education as a foundation for more.

Brief of the Discussion

The affirmative has proved the following:—

I. There is great need for further restriction of immigration.

II. The educational test would accomplish the further restriction of immigration in a proper manner.

Therefore, immigration to the United States should be further restricted by an educational test.

EXERCISES

State the propositions upheld in the following arguments, and put the material into brief form:—

1. At all events, this is clear: that throughout those six months the government knew perfectly well the danger in which General Gordon was placed. It has been said that General Gordon did not ask for troops. Well, I am surprised at that defense. One of the characteristics of General Gordon was the extreme abnegation of his nature. It was not to be expected that he should send home a telegram to say, "I am in great danger, therefore send me troops." He would probably have cut off his right hand before he would have sent such a telegram. But he did send a telegram that the people of Khartum were in danger, and that the Mahdi must win unless military succor was sent forward, and distinctly telling the government — and this is the main point — that unless they would consent to his views the supremacy of the Mahdi was assured.

My lords, is it conceivable that after that — two

Brief of the Discussion

months after that — in May, the prime minister should have said that the government was waiting to have reasonable proof that Gordon was in danger? By that time Khartum was surrounded, and the governor of Berber had announced that his case was desperate, which was too surely proved by the massacre which took place in June.

And yet in May Mr. Gladstone was waiting for reasonable proof that they were in danger. Apparently he did not get that proof till August.

A general sent forward on a dangerous expedition does not like to go whining for assistance, unless he is pressed by absolute peril. All those great qualities which go to make men heroes are such as are absolutely incompatible with such a course, and lead them to shrink as from a great disgrace from any unnecessary appeal for exertion for their protection. It was the business of the government not to interpret General Gordon's telegrams as if they had been statutory declarations, but to judge for themselves of the circumstances of the case, and to see that those who were surrounded, who were the only three Englishmen among this vast body of Mohammedans, who were already cut off from all communication with the civilized world by the occupation of every important town upon the river, were in real danger.

I do not know any other instance in which a man has been sent to maintain such a position without a certain number of British troops. If the British troops had been there treachery would have been impossible; but sending Gordon by himself to rely on the fidelity of Africans and Egyptians was an act of extreme rashness, and if the government succeed in proving, which I do not think they can, that treachery was inevitable, they only pile up an additional reason for their condemnation. I confess it is very difficult to separate this question from the personal matters involved. It is very difficult to argue it on purely abstract grounds without turning for a moment to the character of the man who was engaged and the terrible position in which he was placed.

When we consider all that he underwent, all that he sacrificed in order to save the government in a moment of extreme exigency, there is something infinitely pathetic in reflecting on his feelings, as day after day, week after week, month after month passed by — as he spared no exertions, no personal sacrifice, to perform the duties that were placed upon him — as he lengthened out the siege by inconceivable prodigies of ingenuity, of activity, of resource — and as, in spite of it all, in spite of the deep devotion to his country, which had prompted him to this great risk and undertaking, the conviction gradually grew upon him that his country had abandoned him.

It is terrible to think what he must have suffered when at last, as a desperate measure to save those he loved, he parted with the only two Englishmen with whom during those long months he had any converse, and sent Stewart and Power down the river to escape from the fate which had become inevitable to himself. It is very painful to think of the reproaches to his country and to his country's government that must have passed through the mind of that devoted man during those months of unmerited desertion. In Gordon's letter of the fourteenth of December he said: "All is up. I expect the catastrophe in ten days' time; it would not have been so if our people had kept me better informed as to their intentions."

They had no intentions to inform him of. They were merely acting from hand to mouth to avert the parliamentary censure with which they were threatened. They had no plan, they had no intentions to carry out. If they could have known their intentions, a great hero would have been saved to the British army, a great disgrace

Brief of the Discussion

would not have fallen on the English government.[1]

2. For any State to make sex a qualification that must ever result in the disfranchisement of one entire half of the people is to pass a bill of attainder, or an *ex post facto* law, and is therefore a violation of the supreme law of the land. By it the blessings of liberty are forever witheld from women and their female posterity. To them this government has no just powers derived from the consent of the governed. To them this government is not a democracy. It is not a republic. It is an odious aristocracy; a hateful oligarchy of sex; the most hateful aristocracy ever established on the face of the globe; an oligarchy of wealth, where the rich govern the poor. An oligarchy of learning, where the educated govern the ignorant, or even an oligarchy of race where the Saxon rules the African, might be endured; but this oligarchy of sex, which makes father, brothers, husband, sons, the oligarchs over the mother and sisters, the wife and daughters of every household — which ordains all men sovereigns, all women subjects, carries dissension, discord and rebellion into every home of the nation.

Webster, Worcester and Bouvier all define a citizen to be a person in the United States, entitled to vote and hold office.

The only question left to be settled now is: Are women persons? And I hardly believe any of our opponents will have the hardihood to say they are not. Being persons, then, women are citizens; and no State has a right to make any law, or to enforce any old law, that shall abridge their privileges or immunities. Hence, every discrimination against women in the constitutions and laws of the several States is to-day null and void.[2]

[1] On the Desertion of Gordon in Egypt, Lord Salisbury, The World's Famous Orations. Funk & Wagnalls, Vol. V, p. 111.
[2] On Woman's Right to the Suffrage, Susan B. Anthony. The World's Famous Orations. Funk & Wagnalls, Vol. X, p. 59.

Brief of the Discussion

3. The "Legal Intelligencer" prints the full text of the recent decision of Judge Sulzberger in the cause of Claus & Basher *vs.* the Rapid Transit Company, which deals with a phase of the question concerning the use of the streets in obstructing public travel. The Judge, in denying the plaintiffs a rule for a new trial, put the matter under review into his customary concise logic, as follows:

The plaintiff contends that the direction for defendant was erroneous, because the jury should have been given the opportunity to pass upon the question whether he was or was not negligent in placing his wagon in such a position that it encroached three or four feet upon the transit company's track, without which encroachment the accident could not have happened.

His reasons are as follows:

1. That a driver, for the purpose of watering his horses, has the right to encroach on the trolley track.

2. That even if he has not, it is negligence for a motorman not to stop his car in time to prevent a collision in broad daylight with a conspicuous obstacle like a wagon in front of him.

As to the first point:

An obstruction of the highway which is temporary and partial may be justified in cases of plain, evident necessity, but not where that necessity is argumentative and supposititious: Com. *vs.* Passmore, 1 S. & R. 217; Rex v. Russell, 6 East. 427. There was no necessity on the plaintiff to water his horses in the way he did. Two other ways, both perfectly safe, were open to him. He chose the easiest and the riskiest.

But if there had not been two safe ways open for him, he would still have been guilty of negligence in drawing his wagon across a trolley track, on a busy city street, on which cars were running every minute or two. The primary use of the car track is for public travel, not for watering horses. A permanent watering-trough on a side-

Brief of the Discussion

walk, so constructed as not to be usable without stopping the running of the cars, would be a nuisance. The supposed analogy to the right of an abutter to load and unload a necessary article fails entirely. A passing driver is not in the position of an abutter, the reasonableness of whose action is determined by the degree of momentary necessity, and the limit of whose right is that his obstruction must be temporary. Here, however, the watering-trough and not the driver is in the abutter's position. The watering-trough is a public utility, which every one may use. On a warm day, in a busy city street, hundreds of vehicles may stop there, and the quantity of obstruction is not the time occupied by each, but the sum of the times occupied by all. The effect must necessarily be a serious hindrance to public travel, which might sometimes result in complete stoppage.

To use the thought of Mr. Justice Dean, in Com. *vs.* Forrest, 170 Pa. 47, the law would soon be invoked to decide whether the car track was for the cars or for vehicles stopped thereon for the purpose of watering horses; whether the driver of such vehicles was in the exercise of a lawful right or was a usurper of the rights of others.

In the case of Attorney-General *vs.* the Sheffield Gas Consumers' Company, 19 Eng. Law & Eq. 639, Lord Chancellor Cranworth, considering a similar question, used this illustration: "No doubt that it would be a nuisance, and a very serious nuisance, if a person with a barrel organ, or the bagpipes, were to come and station himself under a person's window all day. But when he is going through a city, you know that he will stop ten minutes at one place and ten minutes at another, and you know he will so go on during the day." The watering-trough, however, is stationary.

As to the second point:

The general rule in Pennsylvania is that contributory

negligence prevents recovery. This rule, it is true, does not apply where the defendant is guilty of "negligence so wanton and gross as to be evidence of voluntary injury"; Wynn *vs.* Allord, 5 W. & S. 525; McKnight *vs.* Ratcliff, 44 Pa. 156. There is, however, nothing in the testimony to indicate that the defendant's motorman did anything wanton. Coming down a steep hill, he failed for a moment to see an obstacle which he had a right to expect would not be on the track. No one says that he did not do his best to prevent the collision after he had seen the wagon.

The question at bottom is one of public policy. Should the motorman anticipate that persons of mature age will station their wagons across the tracks? If the rights of the traveling public are to be preserved, the answer must be in the negative.

4. Aside from the money question, the most serious problem that confronts the people of America to-day is that of rescuing their cities, their States and the federal government, including the federal judiciary, from absolute control of corporate monopoly. How to restore the voice of the citizen in the government of his country; and how to put an end to those proceedings in some of the higher courts which are farce and mockery on one side, and a criminal usurpation and oppression on the other. . . .

In as much as no government can endure in which corrupt greed not only makes the laws, but decides who shall construe them, many of our best citizens are beginning to despair of the republic. Others urge that we should remove the bribe-givers — that is, destroy this overwhelming temptation by having the government take all these monopolies itself and furnish the service which they now furnish, and thus not only save our institutions, but have the great profits which now go into the pockets

Brief of the Discussion

of private corporations turned into the public treasury.
. . .

Let us see what civilized man is doing elsewhere. Take the cities of Great Britain first, for they have the same power of self-government that American cities have. In all that pertains to the comfort and enterprise of the individual we are far in the lead; but in the government of cities we are far behind. Glasgow has to-day nearly one million inhabitants and is one of the great manufacturing and commercial cities of the world. Thirty years ago there was scarcely a city that was in a worse condition. Private corporations furnished it a poor quality of water, taken from the Clyde River, and they charged high rates for it. The city drained into the Clyde, and it became horribly filthy. Private corporations furnished a poor quality of gas, at a high price; and private companies operated the street railroads. Private companies had the same grip on the people there that they have in most American cities. Owing to the development of great shipbuilding and other industries in the valley of the Clyde, the laboring population of Glasgow became very dense and the means of housing the people were miserable. Poorly lighted, poorly ventilated, filthy houses brought high rents. In many cases two families lived in one room. Cleanliness was impossible; the sanitary conditions were frightful and the death rate was high. As for educational facilities, there were none worth mentioning for these people. The condition of the laboring classes was one of degradation and misery; children were growing up mentally, morally and physically diseased; a generation was coming which threatened to be an expense and a menace to the country. It was a great slum city.

But patriotic and public-spirited men came to the front and gave the city the benefit of their services free. In

Brief of the Discussion

fact, none of the high city officials in Great Britain received any pay other than the well being of humanity and the good opinions of their country. The city rid itself of the private companies by buying them and then brought fresh water from the highlands, a distance of sixty miles. It doubled the quantity of water furnished the inhabitants, and reduced the cost to consumers by one-half. And yet the department now yields over two hundred thousand dollars a year net income over all fixed charges.

The municipality, after much difficulty, bought the gas plants and gradually reduced the price of gas from $1.14 to 58 cents, and it now illuminates not only the streets and public places, but all passageways and stairways in flat buildings, experience having shown that a good lamp is almost as useful as a policeman. The total debt of the city for plants, extensions, etc., to illumine perfectly all the city had reached nearly five and a half millions of dollars. Notwithstanding the low price at which gas is sold, this sum has gradually been reduced to less than two and a half millions of dollars out of the earnings of the system, and it will soon be wiped out and the entire revenue go into the city treasury.

The street railways were owned by the city, but, until 1894, they were leased out under an arrangement which paid the city full cost of construction, with interest, besides a yearly income of $750 per street mile. In 1894 the city began to operate the lines itself. The fares were reduced 33 per cent., besides special tickets to laborers, so that the average is under two cents, and over one-third of all fares are one cent each.

The private company had worked its men twelve and fourteen hours a day and paid irregular and unsatisfactory wages. The city at once reduced the number of hours to ten, and fixed a satisfactory scale of wages. And, compared with what it formerly was, the service

Brief of the Discussion

has been greatly improved. In spite of all these acts for the benefit of the public, the roads which had cost the city nothing, now net over all charges for improvements, etc., one-fourth of a million annually. In 1892 the city bought out a private electric light company, and now has the monopoly of furnishing electric light and power. This promises to be a source of enormous revenue for the city. . . .

Manchester has within its narrow limits only a little over half a million people, but within a radius of twenty miles from her city hall there are over three million inhabitants. These have to be considered in discussing Manchester, which is essentially a manufacturing and commercial city. Its history is in many respects a parallel of that of Glasgow. It seemed to be a great city of slums, degradation and misery, and was in the grip of private monopolies.

To-day the city furnishes all the service that is furnished here by private corporations, and does it at about one-half cost. It furnishes gas at fifty-six cents a thousand, and after deducting all that is used to illuminate perfectly the streets and after applying $200,000 a year on the original cost of plants, etc., it still turns $300,000 a year into the public treasury, altho the aim in nearly all English cities is not to make money, but to serve the public.

The city constructed an aqueduct ninety miles to secure pure water and furnishes this for a little more than half what the private company had charged for a poor quality of water. It owns street railways, and besides giving greatly reduced rates and giving half-fare tickets to workingmen, the city derives a large revenue from this source. Like Glasgow and Birmingham, the city owns large cemeteries in which there are separate sections for the different religious denominations, and prices are so arranged that while those who desire to do so can get lots costing from ten to thirty dollars, yet "a decent burial with inscription on stone over a grave can be had at about four dollars for adults and three dollars for children. This charge includes all cemetery fees and expenses."

The city owns the markets and slaughter houses. It has provided parks and swimming baths and, like Birmingham and Glasgow, it maintains large technical schools in which thousands of young men are instructed in the industrial arts and sciences, so as to be able to maintain Manchester's greatness.

Birmingham has over half a million of people, and its experience resembles that of Glasgow and Manchester. Formerly private corporations controlled almost everything and charged very high rates for very poor service, and the sanitary conditions were frightful. But here again municipal statesmen came to the front, the most prominent among whom was The Honorable Joseph Chamberlain, who has since been in the British government.

Not going further into detail, let me say there are at present in the United Kingdom 185 municipalities that supply their inhabitants with water, with gas and electric light, and one-third of the street railway mileage of Great Britain is owned by the municipalities. Leaving out London it amounts to two-thirds. And in most instances in which they do not own the street railways, they have compelled the companies to grant low fares and divide profits.

Every business reason applicable to the municipalities and governments of Europe is applicable here. We want as pure water, as good drainage, as cheap service as they have, and we want the same privilege of supplying ourselves as they exercise; and when it is apparent that, by acting collectively, we can do business more successfully, can serve ourselves better in every way, and can secure for the public treasury these millions which now go into the pockets of grasping individuals, have we not a right to do it? If we find that, in this manner, we can give steadiness to labor, and can elevate its standards and improve the conditions of our people, dare we not do it? Every one of the reforms carried out in England and on the continent met with fierce opposition from the same classes that oppose them here, but the business sense and patriotic impulse of the people prevailed, and I believe, will prevail here.[1]

5. Draw a brief of Beecher's speech found on page 166.

[1] On Municipal and Government Ownership, Altgeld. The World's Famous Orations. Funk & Wagnalls Co., Vol. X, p. 208.

CHAPTER VIII

METHODS OF REFUTATION

A COMPLETE argument consists of two kinds of proof: constructive proof and refutation. Constructive proof is that part of an argument which sets forth direct reasons for belief in a certain proposition; refutation is that part which destroys the reasons for belief in the opposite side.

In general, each of these divisions is of about equal importance, at times the value of one predominating and at times the value of the other. If one is addressing an audience unacquainted with his views or hostile towards them, he is not likely to make much progress in getting his own beliefs accepted until he has, at least in part, shattered the opinion already existing. If, however, the audience is predisposed or even willing to accept the doctrine advocated, very little but constructive proof may be necessary.

In debate, the side that has the burden of proof will usually have more use for constructive argu-

Refutation

ment, and the opposite side will have more use for refutation. This statement will not always hold true, however, for the rule will vary under different circumstances; a debater must, therefore, hold himself in readiness to meet whatever contingencies arise. Debate may be likened to the play of two boys building houses with blocks; each boy builds the best house he can, and at times attempts to overthrow the work of his playmate. The one that has the better structure when the game ends comes off victorious. Thus it is in debate; each debater must do his best both to build up his own argument and to destroy his opponent's.

To handle refutation successfully, either in written argument or in debate, one must know what to refute and what to leave alone. The general rule governing this matter is: *Refute only those arguments which are essential to the proof of the other side.* All trivial ideas, even all misstatements which if refuted would not destroy any fundamental process of an opponent's proof, should pass unnoticed. To mention them means waste of time and effort. It is not uncommon for a debater to make trivial errors intentionally, in the hope that his opponent will consume valuable time in refuting them and thus allow his main argument to go unscathed. When this stratagem succeeds, the one who made the mistakes can acknowledge that he was wrong in those unimportant details, and yet show that his fundamental arguments have not been overthrown. While arguing on a political question, an intercollegiate debater once laid considerable stress on an opinion expressed by Woodrow Wilson, " President," as he stated, " of Harvard University." His opponent, of course, might have held this statement up to ridicule, but such an exposure would have been impolitic, in that it would have in no wise impaired the value of Mr. Wilson's opinion as evidence. Another debater, not so wise, once spent considerable time in correcting an opponent who had said that the Steel Trust was formed in 1891 instead of in 1901, as was the case. As these dates had no vital bearing on the question at issue, the error should have been allowed to pass. The temptation to point out the flaws that are most obvious is always great, but unless by so doing one can knock out the props on which an opponent's proof rests, such an attack accomplishes nothing.

Another common error in refutation consists in " answering one's self." A person is guilty of this fault whenever he misstates an opponent's argument, either because he does not understand it or

Refutation

through design, and then refutes this misstatement. The folly of such procedure is made apparent by merely calling attention to the fact that the original argument has been garbled but in no wise refuted. An opponent can convict the one who has "answered himself" either of unpardonable ignorance about the subject or of downright dishonesty.

To guard against these errors of refuting unimportant details and of "answering one's self," it is always well to reduce an opponent's argument to the form of a brief. If the argument is in print, this task is comparatively simple; if the argument is oral, the task will be harder but will still present no serious difficulties to one who is used to drawing briefs. When all the ideas have been arranged in the form of headings and subheadings, and the relation between the ideas has been indicated by means of numbers and letters, then the arguer can quickly decide what points he ought to refute and what ones he can refute.

It goes without saying that the headings marked with the Roman numerals contain the most important ideas, and should, therefore, be overthrown as far as possible. There are three ways of disposing of them: one way is to state that the headings are false and then bring on new proof to show

Refutation

their falsity; the second way is to call attention to the subheadings with which the opponent has bolstered up the main headings, and then, by proving these subheads false, allow the main heads to fall to the ground; the third way is to admit that the subheads are true and then show that the inferences drawn from them are unwarranted.

To illustrate: A part of an argument on the affirmative side of the proposition, " *Resolved,* That students in American colleges should be excused from final examinations in all subjects in which they have attained a daily grade of at least eighty-five per cent.," might be reduced to the following brief form:—

I. This rule would be of great intellectual benefit to college students, for

    A. They would master their work more thoroughly, because

        1. They would study harder during the term.

The first method of overthrowing the heading indicated by (I) would be to attack it directly. This attack might consist of opinions of prominent educators who, on theoretical grounds, do not believe an intellectual benefit would result from the adoption of such a rule; of the opinions of edu-

Refutation

cators who have tried the rule and declare that it is an intellectual detriment; and of a course of reasoning which would show that this system would rob the students exempted of the great intellectual benefit that is derived from the preparation for an examination and from the taking of an examination.

The second method would be to show that (1) is not true; therefore (A) would be false, and (I) would be left entirely unsupported.

Under the third method the arguer would admit the truth of (1), but would deny that the truth of (A) is established by it; therefore (I) would be unsupported.

Whenever a subheading is attacked, it is always very essential to show that the attack is made simply because this subheading serves as a foundation for the main heading. In this particular argument, refutation according to the second and third methods might read about as follows: "The contention of the affirmative that the eighty-five per cent. rule should be adopted because it would result in an intellectual improvement among college students, rests on the supposition that students would study harder during the term, and for that reason would more thoroughly master their subjects. This reasoning is erroneous because, in the first place, as I will show, but very few students, if any, would study harder during the term; and, in the second place, even if they did, those exempted would not have mastered their work so completely at the end of the year as they would have if they had taken an examination."

From the preceding, it is apparent that refutation consists of discrediting evidence and attacking reasoning. The ways to overthrow evidence will be considered first.

EVIDENCE.

It is taken for granted that the evidence mustered by the opponent is sufficient, if not overthrown, to establish his side of the discussion. Of course, if enough evidence for this purpose is lacking, one has only to call attention to this fundamental weakness in order to overthrow the argument then and there. The rules, therefore, for testing evidence assume that the opponent has cited facts that, if not combated, will establish his case.

These tests are the same as those given in Chapter VI; a hasty review of them, however, may be serviceable at this point.

Refutation

I. Tests of the sources of evidence.

    A. Is the witness competent to give a trustworthy account of the matter?

    B. Is the witness willing to give an accurate account?

        1. Does he have any personal interest in the case?

    C. Is the witness prejudiced?

    D. Does the witness have a good reputation for honesty and accuracy?

II. Internal tests of evidence.

    A. Is the evidence consistent (a) with itself, (b) with known facts, (c) with human experience?

    B. Is it first-hand evidence?

    C. Can the evidence be classed as especially valuable?

        1. Does it consist of hurtful admissions?

        2. Is it undesigned evidence?

        3. Is it negative evidence?

III. Test of argument from authority.

    A. Is the witness an acknowledged authority on the subject about which he testifies?

To overthrow or weaken argument from authority, one may either discredit its source or bring to

Refutation

light some inconsistency in the statement itself. Usually the former method alone is possible. To accomplish this result, one may show that the witness spoke from insufficient knowledge of the matter, or was prejudiced, or had some personal interest in the case. Counter authority will also be of assistance. The following quotation taken from a college debate furnishes the student a good example of how to handle this sort of refutation.

"The argument has been advanced that the South does not need the foreign laborer, and this argument has been supported by the words of Mr. Prescott F. Hall. We would call the attention of the audience and the judges to the fact that since Prescott F. Hall is Secretary of the Immigration Restriction League, it would be to his interest to make this assertion. Why do not our opponents refer to impartial and unprejudiced men, men like Dr. Allen McLaughlin, a United States immigration official, who makes just the opposite statement?"

REASONING.

I. Induction.

    A. Have enough instances of the class under consideration been investigated to es-

Refutation

tablish the existence of a general law?

    B.   Have enough instances been investigated to establish the probable existence of a general law?

II. Deduction.

    A.   Are both premises true?

    B.   Is the fact stated in the minor premise an instance of the general law expressed in the major premise?

III. Antecedent probability.

    A.   Is the assigned cause of sufficient strength to produce the alleged effect?

    B.   May some other cause intervene and prevent the action of the assigned cause?

IV. Sign.

    A.   Argument from effect to cause.

        1.   Is the assigned cause adequate to produce the observed effect?

        2.   Could the observed effect have resulted from any other cause than the one assigned?

    B.   Argument from effect to effect.

        1.   Do the combined tests of argument from effect to cause and from cause to effect hold?

Refutation

V. Example.
    A. Is there any fundamental difference be-
        tween the case in hand and the case
        cited as an example?

FALLACIES.

A fallacy is an error in reasoning. The preceding part of this chapter has already suggested tests
that will expose many such faults, but there are a
few errors which, because of their frequency or
their inadaptability to other classification, demand
separate treatment. This book follows the plan of
most other texts on argumentation, and treats these
errors under a separate head marked fallacies. To
detect a fallacy in another's argument is to weaken,
if not to destroy, his case; to avoid making a fallacy in one's own argument means escape from hu-
miliation and defeat. Hence, a knowledge of fallacies is one of the most essential parts of a debater's
equipment.

The classification given here does not pretend to
be exhaustive; it does, however, consider the most
common and insidious breaches of reasoning that
are likely to occur, and the following pages should
be studied with great care.

Refutation

I. Begging the Question. (Petitio Principii.)

1. Mere assumption.

Begging the question means assuming the truth of that which needs proof. This fallacy is found in its simplest form in epithets and appellations. The lawyer who speaks of " the criminal on trial for his life," begs the question in that he assumes the prisoner to be a criminal before the court has rendered a verdict. Those writers who have recently discussed " the brutal game of football " without having first adduced a particle of proof to show that the game is brutal, fall into the same error. An unpardonable instance of question-begging lies in the following introduction, once given by a debater who was attacking the proposition, *" Resolved,* That the federal government should own and operate the railroads in the United States ":—

"We of the negative will show that the efficient and highly beneficial system of private ownership should be maintained, and that the impracticable system of government ownership can never succeed in the United States or in any similarly governed country."

Private ownership and government ownership may possess these qualities attributed to them, but the debater has no right to make such an assump-

Refutation

tion; he must *prove* that they have these qualities.

2. Assumption used as proof. Such barefaced assumptions as the preceding usually do little damage except to the one who makes them. They are not likely to lead astray an audience of average intelligence; on the other hand, they do stamp the arguer as prejudiced and illogical. But when assumptions are used as proof, hidden in the midst of quantities of other material, they may produce an unwarranted effect upon one who is not a clear thinker, or who is off his guard. If, without showing that football is brutal, one calls it an extremely brutal game, and then urges its abolishment on the ground of its brutality, he has used an assumption as proof, and has, therefore, begged the question. The debater who stated, without proving, that vast numbers of unskilled laborers were needed in the United States, and then urged this as a reason why no educational test should be applied to immigrants coming to this country, furnished an example of the same fallacy.

3. Unwarranted assumption of the truth of a suppressed premise. The student is already familiar with the enthymeme. The enthymeme constitutes a valid form of reasoning only when the suppressed premise is recognized as true.

Refutation

Therefore, whenever an arguer makes use of the enthymeme without attempting to establish a suppressed premise whose truth is not admitted, he has argued fallaciously. This is a third method of begging the question. To illustrate: In advocating the abolishment of football from the list of college athletic sports, one might reason, " Football should be abolished because it obviously exposes a player to possible injury." The suppressed premise in this case would be: All sports which expose a player to possible injury should be abolished. Failure to prove the truth of this unadmitted statement constitutes the fallacy.

4. **Assumption equivalent to the proposition to be proved.** It is not surprising that a man carried away with excitement or prejudice should make assumptions that he does not even try to substantiate, but that anyone should assume the truth of the very conclusion that he has set out to establish seems incredible. Such a form of begging the question, however, does frequently occur. Sometimes the fallacy is so hidden in a mass of illustration and rhetorical embellishment that at first it is not apparent; but stripped of its verbal finery, it stands out very plainly. The following passage written on the affirmative side of the proposition,

223

Refutation

"*Resolved,* That the college course should be shortened to three years," will serve as a particularly flagrant illustration :—

> It is a well-known fact that in the world of to-day time is an essential factor in the race for success. No young man can afford to dawdle for four long years in acquiring a so-called "higher" education. Three-fourths of that time is, if anything, more than sufficient in which to attain all the graces and culture that the progressive man needs.

It is evident that the "argument" in this case consists of nothing more than a repetition of the proposition.

5. Arguing in a circle. Another phase of begging the question consists of using an assumption as proof of a proposition and of then quoting the proposition as proof of the assumption. Two assertions are made, neither of which is substantiated by any real proof, but each of which is used to prove the other. This fallacy probably occurs most frequently in conversation. Consider the following :—

A. "The proposed system of taxation is an excellent one."

B. "What makes you think so?"

A. "Because it will be adopted by the legislature."

Refutation

B. "How do you know it will?"

A. "Because it is a good system and our legislators are men of sense."

This fallacy occurs when one proves the authority of the church from the testimony of the scriptures, and then establishes the authenticity of the scriptures by the testimony of the church. A similar fallacy has been pointed out in the works of Plato. In *Phædo,* he demonstrates the immortality of the soul from its simplicity, and in the *Republic,* he demonstrates the simplicity of the soul from its immortality. The following fragment of a brief argues in a circle:—

I. This principle is in accordance with the principles of the Democratic party, since

    A. The leader of the Democratic party believes in it, for

        1. As the leader of the party, he naturally believes in Democratic principles.

II. Ambiguous Terms. (Equivocation; Confusion of Terms.)

The fallacy of ambiguous terms consists of using the same term in two distinct senses in the same argument. Thus if one were to argue that "no designing person ought to be trusted; engravers are by profession designers; therefore they ought not to be trusted," it is quite apparent that the term "design" means totally different things in the two premises. The same fallacy occurs in the argument, "Since the American people believe in a republican form of government, they should vote the Republican ticket." Again :—

"Interference with another man's business is illegal;

"Underselling interferes with another man's business;

"Therefore underselling is illegal."

J. S. Mill in his *System of Logic* discusses the fallacy of ambiguous terms with great care. In part he says :—

The mercantile public are frequently led into this fallacy by the phrase "scarcity of money." In the language of commerce, "money" has two meanings: *currency,* or the circulating medium; and *capital seeking investment,* especially investment on loan. In this last sense, the word is used when the "money market" is spoken of, and when the "value of money" is said to be high or low, the rate of interest being meant. The consequence of this ambiguity is, that as soon as scarcity of money in the latter of these senses begins to be felt,— as soon as there is difficulty of obtaining loans, and the rate of interest is high,— it is concluded that this must arise from causes acting upon the quantity of money in the other and more popular sense; that the circulating medium must have diminished in quantity, or ought to be increased. I am aware that, independently of the double meaning of the term, there are in the facts themselves some peculiarities, giving an apparent support to this error; but the ambiguity of the language stands on the very threshold of the subject, and intercepts all attempts to throw light upon it.

As countless words and expressions have several meanings, there is almost no limit to the confusion which this fallacy can cause. Some of the most common terms that are used ambiguously are *right, liberty, law, representative, theory, church, state, student.*

By carefully defining all terms that have more than one meaning and by insisting on a rigid adherence to the one meaning wherever the term is used, a debater can easily avoid fallacies of this sort in his own argument and expose those of his opponent.

III.   False Cause.

The fallacy of false cause occurs whenever that which could in no way bring about the effect that is being established is urged as its cause. This fallacy in its most obvious form is found only in the arguments of careless and illogical thinkers. Some College students occasionally draw briefs

Refutation

that contain such reasoning as the following:—

I. The Panama canal should be of the sea-level rather
than of the lock type, because
   A. The Panama canal will do away with the long
   voyage around the Horn.

I. Southerners are justified in keeping the franchise
away from the negro, for
   A. Negroes should never have been brought to America.
   B. The Fifteenth Amendment to the Constitution
   ought not to have been passed.

The error of such plainly absurd reasoning as
occurs in the preceding illustrations needs no explanation. There is one form of the fallacy of
false cause, however, that is much more common
and insidious and therefore deserves special treatment.

Post hoc ergo propter hoc. (After this, therefore, on account of this.) This phase of the fallacy
consists of the assumption that since cause precedes effect what has preceded an event has caused
it. The most frequent occurrence of the error is
to be found in superstitions. If some one meets
with an accident while taking a journey that began
on Friday, many people will argue that the accident
is the effect of the unlucky day. Some farmers believe their crops will not prosper unless the planting

228

Refutation

is done when the moon is in a certain quarter; sailors often refuse to embark in a renamed vessel. Because in the past, one event has been known to follow another, it is argued that the first event was the cause of the second, and that the second event will invariably follow the first.

But this fallacy does not find its only expression in superstitions. To *post hoc* reasoning is due much of the popularity of patent medicines. Political beliefs, even, are often generated in the same way; prosperity follows the passing of a certain law, and people jump to the conclusion that this one law has caused the "good times." Some demagogues go so far as to say that education among the Indians is responsible for the increased death rate of many of the tribes.

A slightly different phase of the *post hoc* fallacy consists in attributing the existence of a certain condition to a single preceding event, when at the most this event could have been only a partial cause of what followed, and may not have been a cause at all. A medicine that could not have effected a cure may have been of some slight benefit. A law that could not possibly have been the sole cause of "good times" may have had a ben-

Refutation

eficial effect. To avoid this fallacy, one must be sure not only that the assigned cause is operative, but that it is also adequate.

In the following passage, *Harper's Weekly,* for March 5, 1894, points out the error in the reasoning made by several college presidents who, after compiling statistics, stated that a college education increased a man's chance of success from one in ten thousand to one in forty:—

Not many persons doubt any longer that an American college education is an advantage to most youths who can get it, but in these attempts to estimate statistically what college education does for men there is a good deal of confusing of *post hoc* and *propter hoc*. Define success as you will, a much larger proportion of American college men win it than of men who don't go to college, but how much college training does for those successful men is still debatable. Remember that they are a picked lot, the likeliest children of parents whose ability or desire to send their children to college is evidence of better fortune, or at least of higher aspirations than the average. And because their parents are, as a rule, more or less prosperous and well educated, they get and would get, whether they went to college or not, a better than average start in life. . . .

If one boy out of a family of four goes to college, it is the clever one. The boys who might go to college and don't are commonly the lazy ones who won't study. The colleges get nowadays a large proportion of the best boys of the strongest families. The best boys of the strongest families would win far more than their

Refutation

proportionate share of success even if there were no colleges.

An exposure of similarly fallacious reasoning is made by Edward M. Shepard in *The Atlantic Monthly* for October, 1904.

The Republican argument is that the whole edifice of our prosperity depends upon high protective or prohibitive duties, and that to them is due our industrial progress. Is it not, indeed, a disparagement of the self-depending faculties of the American people thus to affirm that, in spite of their marvelous advantages, they would have failed in industrial life unless by force of law they could have prevented the competition with them of other peoples? It is only by the sophistry to which I have referred that this disparagement is justified. It is that old argument of veritable folly that, because event Z follows event W, as it follows events A and B and many besides A, therefore W is the sole cause of Z. Theory or no theory, the Republican says that we have in fact grown rich by protection, because in our country prosperity and protective duties have existed together. They ignore every inconvenient fact. They would have us forget that each of the industrial depressions of 1873–78 and 1893–96 followed long operation of a high protective tariff. They ignore the contribution of soil and climate to our prosperity, the vast increase which modern inventions and improved carrying facilities have, the world over, brought to the productivity of labor, and here in the United States have brought more than anywhere else. They ignore the superior skill and alertness of the American workman and the wonderful extent to which he has been stimulated by the conditions and ideals of our democracy. They ignore the freedom of trade, which, since 1789, the

Refutation

Federal Constitution has made operative over our entire country,— by far the most important area of free trade ever known,— and which everyone to-day knows to be a prime condition of the prosperity of our forty-five commonwealths.

From what has been said it is obvious that it is never safe to account for an occurrence or a condition by merely referring to something that accompanies it or precedes it. There must be a connection between the alleged cause and the effect, and this connection must be causal; otherwise, both may be the result of the same cause. The cause must also be adequate; and it must, moreover, be evident that the result has not been produced, wholly or partially, by some other cause or causes.

IV. Composition and Division.

Composition. The fallacy of composition consists of attributing to a whole that which has been proved only of a part. To condemn or to approve of a fraternity because of the conduct of only a few of its members, to say that what is advantageous for certain states in the Union would therefore be beneficial for the United States as a whole, to reason from the existence of a few millionaires that the English nation is wealthy, would be to fall into this fallacy. Furthermore, it is fallacious to

Refutation

think that because something is true of each member of a class taken *distributively,* the same thing holds true of the class taken *collectively.* It is not logical to argue that because each member of a jury is very likely to judge erroneously, the jury as a whole is also very likely to judge erroneously. Because each witness to an event is liable to give false or incorrect evidence, it is unreasonable to think that no confidence can be placed in the concurrent testimony of a number of witnesses.

Division. The fallacy of division is the converse of the fallacy of composition. It consists of attributing to a part that which has been proved of the whole. For instance, Lancaster county is the most fertile county in Pennsylvania, but that fact by itself does not warrant the statement that any one particular farm is exceptionally fertile. Because the people of a country are suffering from famine, it does not follow that one particular person is thus afflicted. Again, it would be fallacious to say: It is admitted that the judges of the court of appeal cannot misinterpret the law; Richard Rowe is a judge of the court of appeal; therefore he cannot misinterpret the law.

Refutation

V. Ignoring the Question. (Ignoratio Elenchi.)

An arguer is said to ignore the question, or to argue beside the point, whenever he attempts to prove or disprove anything except the proposition under discussion. This fallacy may arise through carelessness or trickery. An unskilled debater will often unconsciously wander away from his subject; and an unscrupulous debater, when unable to defend his position, will sometimes cunningly shift his ground and argue upon a totally new proposition, which is, however, so similar to the original one that in the heat of controversy the change is hardly noticeable. A discussion on the subject, " The boycott is a legitimate means of securing concessions from employers," which attempted to show the effectiveness of the boycott, would ignore the question. Likewise, in a discussion on the proposition, " The average college student could do in three years the work now done in four," any proof showing the desirability of such a crowding together of college work would be *beside the point*.

In the following passage Macaulay holds up to scorn certain arguments which contain this fallacy :—

Refutation

The advocates of Charles, like the advocates of other malefactors against whom overwhelming evidence is produced, generally decline all controversy about facts, and content themselves with calling testimony to character. We charge him with having broken his coronation oath; and we are told that he kept his marriage vow! We accuse him of having given up his people to the merciless inflictions of the most hot-headed and hard-hearted of prelates; and the defence is, that he took his little son on his knees and kissed him! We censure him for having violated the articles of the Petition of Rights, after having, for good and valuable consideration, promised to obey them; and we are informed that he was accustomed to hear prayers at six o'clock in the morning!

Whenever an arguer avoids the question at issue and makes an attack upon the character, principles, or former beliefs or personal peculiarities of his opponent, he commits the special form of this fallacy known as *argumentum ad hominem*. It is obviously fallacious to reason that a principle is unsound because it is upheld by an untrustworthy advocate, or because it is inconsistent with the advocate's former beliefs and practices. Honesty is a worthy principle, even though advocated by a thief. The duty of industry is no less binding because it is advocated by an idler. Lawyers often commit this error by seeking to discredit the opposing attorney. Campaign speakers frequently attempt to overthrow the opposing party's platform

Refutation

by showing that it is inconsistent with the party's previous measures and declarations. To bring in such irrelevant matter is to ignore the question.

Closely allied to *argumentum ad hominem* is another phase of ignoring the question called *argumentum ad populum*. This fallacy consists of using before a certain audience statements which will strongly appeal to their prejudices and partisan views, but which are not generally accepted facts and which would undoubtedly meet with strong opposition elsewhere. A speaker who brings in this kind of argument makes use neither of reasoning nor of legitimate persuasion. He neglects his proposition and attempts to excite the feelings of his audience to such an extent as to render them incapable of forming a dispassionate judgment upon the matter in hand.

In general, it is necessary only to point out a fallacy to weaken an argument. Sometimes, however, the error is so involved and so hidden that, though it is apparent to one who is arguing, yet it is not easily made apparent to the audience. In overcoming this difficulty, arguers often resort to certain peculiar devices of arranging and presenting the material for refutation. Long experience

Refutation

has shown that the two methods given here are of inestimable value.

I. Reductio ad Absurdum. (Reducing to an Absurdity.)

The method of refuting an argument by *reductio ad absurdum* consists of showing that the argument to be refuted, if true, proves not only the conclusion given, but also other conclusions which are manifestly absurd. For example, a debater once contended that colleges should not seek to root out professionalism in athletic sports, because, by coming in contact with college life, professional players receive considerable benefit. His opponent answered him by showing that the same argument carried out to its logical conclusion would prove that a college should encourage the attendance of criminals and degenerates on the ground that they will be benefited thereby. Thus he reduced the argument to a manifest absurdity.

At one time the officers of a national bank permitted their institution to be wrecked by certifying, and thereby practically guaranteeing, the checks of a firm of stock-holders when the brokers did not have the money represented by the checks deposited in the bank. This was distinctly a criminal offense. The brokers failed, and, the bank having closed its doors in consequence, the president of the bank was brought to trial. *The Atlantic Monthly* reduces to an absurdity the chief argument used for the defense.

A jury having been empaneled to try him, he pleaded guilty, his counsel urging, as a reason for clemency, that the violation of this statute was a habit of the New York banks in the Wall Street district, and that if the wrecked bank had not followed this law-breaking custom of its competitors the stock brokers would have withdrawn their account. The plea was successful, and the officer escaped with a small fine. Imagine a burglar or a pickpocket urging a plea for clemency based on the general business habits and customs of his criminal confrères! [1]

Mr. E. A. Freeman, the historian, once made the statement that English literature cannot be taught. His course of reasoning was to the effect that it is impossible to teach a subject in which one cannot be examined; and he maintained that it is impossible to hold satisfactory examinations in English literature, since this is a subject which is studied for the purpose of cultivating the taste, educating the sympathies, and enlarging the mind. If this reasoning proves anything, it has been pointed out, it proves too much. What Mr. Freeman says of

[1] The Atlantic Monthly, Vol. 94, p. 173.

Refutation

English literature may equally well be said of Latin, Greek, and every other kind of literature. But as Latin and Greek literature have been successfully taught for hundreds of years, Mr. Freeman's argument is absurd.

College students are continually urging as a defense of professionalism in their own athletic teams the argument that since other colleges employ professional players it is necessary for them to do likewise. By carrying this argument a step farther, one could show, with equal reason, that since drinking, stealing and cheating are prevalent in other colleges, these same practices should also be indulged in at the college in question. In the same way one may refute by *reductio ad absurdum* all such arguments as, "Custom has rendered the spoils system desirable"; "The prevalency of the high license law shows its superiority to prohibition"; and "Since in the past all college students were required to study Latin and Greek, these subjects should be required at the present time."

II. The Dilemma.

Another device an arguer will often find useful in refuting an opponent's statement is the *dilemma*.

Refutation

In the dilemma the arguer shows that the statement he wishes to disprove can be true only through the truth of at least one of several possibilities. He then proves that these possibilities are untenable, and therefore the original statement is false. To represent the dilemma with letters: The truth of A rests upon the truth of either x or y; but as x and y are both false, A is false. Once when it was believed in certain quarters that Japan was about to undertake a war against the United States, many people maintained that if Japan desired to go to war she was amply able to finance such an undertaking. In reply to this contention, a certain newspaper, making use of the dilemma, said that since Japan had no money in the treasury she could meet the expenses of war in only three ways: either by contracting a large debt, or by increasing taxation, or by indemnifying herself at the expense of the enemy. The paper then went on to prove that Japan was not in a position to float a large loan, that taxes in Japan were already as heavy as the people could bear, and that she could not hope, at least for a long time, to secure any indemnity from the enemy. Therefore Japan was not in a financial position to enter upon a war with the United States.

Refutation

In attempting to show that municipalities do not have the moral right to own and operate public utilities, T. Carpenter Smith uses the dilemma. He says:—

"Any commercial business is carried on either at a profit, or at a loss, or in such a way that the expenses equal the income. If the city business of gas or electric lighting is to be carried on at a profit, then those citizens who use gas or electric light will be charged a high price for that light, in order to pay the profit, not only to themselves, but also to those who do not use it. If the works are to be carried on at a loss, then the citizens who do not use the gas or electric light will pay taxes to furnish a convenience or economy to those citizens who do use it. If the works are to be operated exactly at cost, then the city will carry on a business from which it will get nothing, but in which it will have to take the labor and risk incident to such a business in order to benefit only some of its citizens, furnishing a commodity not desired by all."

In conversation and debate, the dilemma is frequently introduced by means of a question. The debater, wishing to trap his opponent, asks him a pertinent question which previous investigation has shown can possibly be answered in only two or three ways, and which the opponent cannot afford to answer at all. A good illustration of this device occurs in the New Testament.

And it came to pass, on one of the days, as he was teaching the people in the temple, and preaching the

Refutation

gospel, there came upon him the chief priests and the scribes with the elders; and they spake, saying unto him, Tell us: By what authority doest thou these things? or who is he that gave thee this authority? And he answered and said unto them, I also will ask you a question; and tell me: The baptism of John, was it from heaven, or from men? And they reasoned with themselves, saying, If we shall say, From heaven; he will say, Why did ye not believe him? But if we shall say, From men; all the people will stone us: for they be persuaded that John was a prophet. And they answered, that they knew not whence *it was*. And Jesus said unto them, Neither tell I you by what authority I do these things.[1]

During the Lincoln-Douglas debates in 1858, when both men were seeking the United States senatorship from Illinois, Lincoln, wishing either to kill Douglas's senatorial prospects or to head him off from the presidency two years later, asked him a question which put him in a dilemma. Ida M. Tarbell describes the question as follows:—

"Can the people of a United States territory in any lawful way, against the wish of any citizen of the United States, exclude slavery from its limits prior to the formation of a State Constitution?" Lincoln had seen the irreconcilableness of Douglas's own measure of popular sovereignty, which declared that the people of a territory should be left to regulate their domestic concerns in their own way subject only to the Constitution, and the decision of the Supreme Court in the Dred Scott case that slaves, being property, could not under the Constitution be excluded from a territory. He knew that if

[1] Luke xx, 1–8.

242

Refutation

Douglas said *no* to this question, his Illinois constituents would never return him to the Senate. He believed that if he said *yes,* the people of the South would never vote for him for President of the United States.

In the last example, Lincoln, by forcing Douglas to answer this question, sought to destroy, and, as history shows, did destroy, the popular conception of Douglas's fitness for public office.

Before one can safely use the dilemma he must carefully investigate every phase of the statement that he wishes to refute. If he is to use the dilemma directly, he must consider every possibility — commonly called the horns of the dilemma — upon which the truth of the statement may rest. If there is a single possibility which he is not ready to meet and overthrow, his whole effort is fruitless. For instance, a debater, in attempting to rebut the statement that college fraternities are harmful, said that his opponent must show that fraternities are either morally, socially, financially or intellectually detrimental to their members; he then proved as best he could that in these respects fraternities are beneficial rather than harmful, and sat down thinking that he had gone a long way toward winning the debate. His opponent then arose and admitting nearly everything that had been said, based his argument on the idea that fraternities were harmful

to the college as a whole. The first speaker had
not considered every alternative. If an arguer is to
approach a dilemma through the medium of a question, he must be sure that he knows every reasonable answer that his opponent can make. When
one has satisfied these conditions, he can use the
dilemma with great effect.

By way of summary it may be said that the successful arguer must both build up his own proof
and destroy his opponent's. To accomplish the latter one has to know what to refute and what to
leave alone; he must distinguish between the important and the unessential, and he must take care
not to " refute himself." Since proof consists of
evidence and reasoning, the first step for him to
take in refuting an argument is to apply the tests
for each, and if possible show where his opponent
has erred. In the next place, he should see whether
he can discover and point out any of the more important fallacies; the ones mentioned here are *beg-*
ging the question, ambiguous terms, false cause,
composition and division, and *ignoring the ques-*
tion. Should the arguer find any of these fundamental weaknesses, it is ordinarily sufficient merely
to call attention to them; for the sake of emphasis,
however, one may make use of two especially ef-

Refutation

fective methods of refutation, *reductio ad absurdum*
and the *dilemma.*

EXERCISES.

A. Criticize the following arguments and point out the
fallacies they contain :—

1. Four thousand men have taken examinations at
Princeton under the honor system, and only six of these
were found guilty of " cribbing." This record shows conclusively that the honor system restrains dishonest work
in examinations.

2. Athletics do not injure a man's scholarship; one of
the best players on last year's football team attained such
a high grade that he was awarded a fellowship.

3. During the decade from 1870 to 1880, illiteracy among
the negroes decreased ten per cent., but the race grew
more criminal by twenty-five per cent.; from 1880 to
1890, illiteracy decreased eighteen per cent., but criminality
increased thirty-three and one-third per cent. Who can
now say that education does not injure the negro?

4. Since the honor system failed at Franklin and Mar-
shall, it will fail at —— College.

5. Frequent athletic games benefit a college because
they tend to take the students' attention away from their
studies.

6. The fixed curriculum of studies is effective in making a specialist, because the specialist takes up only one
kind of work.

7. Southerners are justified in keeping the franchise
from the negro, because the Fifteenth Amendment to the
Constitution ought never to have been passed.

8. Since the negro's devotion to the church is as great
as that of most white people, he is of as high moral standing as the average unintelligent white.

9. Ireland is idle and therefore she starves; she starves
and therefore she rebels.

Refutation

10. Every one desires virtue, because every one desires happiness.

11. The present term of four years is so short a time that the President does not have opportunity to become acquainted with his duties, for just as he is becoming acquainted with them he has to step out of office.

12. This doctrine cannot be proved from the Gospels, nor from the Acts of the Apostles, nor from the Epistles, nor from the Revelation of St. John; therefore it cannot be proved from the New Testament.

13. Crime is a violation of the laws of our country; piracy is a crime; this man belongs to a band of lawless men, and this band has been taken in the very deed of piracy. Therefore he has violated the laws of our country.

14. Since all presuming men are contemptible, and since this man presumes to believe his opinions are correct, he is not worthy of our consideration.

15. To prove to you that our standing army should be permanently enlarged, I will show that every nation of any prominence whatsoever keeps a standing army.

16. The elective system of studies is preferable to the prescribed system, because
    A. The student can elect those studies which will do him the most good, for
        1. He can elect what he pleases.

17. Strikes benefit the working man, because
    A. They benefit him financially, for
        1. If they did not, he would not strike.

18. When thirteen sit at table together, one of them always dies within the year.

19. To decide whether or not strikes are justifiable it is necessary to see if they have for the most part been successful in the past.

20. All the trees in the park make a thick shade; this is one of them, therefore this tree makes a thick shade.

Refutation

21. Italy is a Catholic country and abounds in beggars; France is also a Catholic country, and therefore abounds in beggars.

22. Pitt was not a great and useful minister; for though he would have been so had he carried out Adam Smith's doctrines of free trade, he did not carry out those doctrines.

23. All criminal actions ought to be punished by law. Prosecutions for theft are criminal actions, and therefore ought to be punished by law.

24. Books are a source both of instruction and of amusement; a table of logarithms is a book; therefore it is a source both of instruction and of amusement.

B. On each of the following arguments from authority write a paragraph that will weaken its effect:—

1. "The Senate for more than a century has demonstrated the wisdom of the mode of its constitution." Senator G. F. Hoar.

2. "Mine disasters are largely due to the intoxication of miners, or to carelessness caused by the after effects of a 'spree,'" says Dr. Jesse K. Johnson, superintendent of one of the largest mines in the Pittsburg district.

3. Both Mark Hanna and Grover Cleveland have stated that a six year Presidential term would be of great benefit to the United States.

4. Senator La Follet, who has made a thorough study of many of the principal monopolies in the country, states that the Standard Oil trust charges exorbitant rates.

5. Mr. Francis Walker, in the Political Science Quarterly, Volume twenty, page fourteen, says that legislation against trusts has improved conditions, and would therefore improve conditions in the United States.

6. President Hadley, of Yale University, has said that the subsidizing of ships on a large scale has been detrimental to France.

Refutation

7. " The Indian who is not obliged to labor for his maintenance becomes a lazy vagabond." Lyman Abbott.

C. Put the following article into the form of a brief and show exactly what methods of refutation are used :—

The old frigate " Constitution."

The pretexts for removal of " Old Ironsides " from the waters in which that historic ship had her birth are now reduced to two.

One of these is that the old boat takes up room at the Navy Yard which is needed for the work of that establishment.

The other is that since the money expended in the restoration of the frigate — less than $200,000 — came out of the Federal Treasury, the people of distant States ought to have the pleasure of seeing what their money paid for without coming to Boston in order to enjoy it.

As for crowding the Navy Yard, that is an absurdity. His Excellency Curtis Guild, Jr., in his letter to the Navy Department protesting against the removal, quoted the officers in command at the Navy Yard as declaring that " the ship in no way interferes with the work of the yard, taking up no space that is needed for other purposes." The Governor would not make such a statement in an official communication without the clearest authority. " Indeed," he adds as his own opinion, " the strip of wharf occupied is but a trivial portion of the long water front controlled by the government."

There is the other pretext, namely, that because the " Constitution " has been repaired at national cost, therefore any special claim that Massachusetts may have upon this relic of Massachusetts patriotism is removed. This idea has found crude and unmannerly expression in the words of one of the committee of Congress looking over our navy yards. " The agitation to keep the ship in Boston seems selfish," he is quoted as saying. " It was the

Refutation

money of the whole people of the United States that paid for its repair, and the people in other sections are as justly entitled to see the ship as in Boston."

Coming from a representative of the State of Kansas, this is almost amusing. His proposition to tow the ship around from place to place, as it may be wanted for a show, suggests the practicability of a canal, say, to Topeka, or to Fort Hayes.

The alternative proposition, namely, that Massachusetts shall repay to the general government the cost of the repairs of the "Constitution," would have some standing were it a commercial affair. Massachusetts has expended many times the cost of the repairs of "Old Ironsides" in preserving for the nation the revolutionary sites and monuments upon our soil. Payment for the repair and restoration of "Old Ironsides" would be a bagatelle if the people of the United States were to demand that this monument also shall be purchased by the people of Massachusetts under threat of its removal.

But it is not a question of money; that is a contemptible suggestion. Nor is it a question of bureaucracy. It is a simple, reasonable, entirely practical demand of the historic sentiment of patriotism which still warms the hearts and inspires the souls of Massachusetts men.

CHAPTER IX

DEBATE — SOME PRACTICAL SUGGESTIONS

DEBATE has been defined as the oral presentation of argument under conditions that allow both sides to be heard. In both class room and intercollegiate debating each side usually makes two speeches, a main speech and a rebuttal speech. The main speech ordinarily extends over a period of from seven to twelve minutes, according to the rules governing the contest, and is largely constructive in nature. The rebuttal speech, commonly called *the rebuttal,* is usually a little less than half the length of the main speech, and is for the most part destructive. It is almost superfluous to add that both sides are allowed exactly the same amount of time in which to present their arguments; that the affirmative side speaks first, the order being, when there are several debaters, affirmative, negative, affirmative, negative, and so on; and that all the main speeches are given before either side makes a rebuttal speech. If there be only one debater on each side, it is undoubtedly best for the affirmative to offer the first rebuttal; if there be several debaters, the order is usually reversed. The debaters on either side may or may not speak in rebuttal in the same order as in the main argument.

HOW TO PREPARE FOR DEBATE.

In several ways the work of the debater differs from the work of one who is preparing a written argument or who is to speak without being confronted by an opponent. As far as the completion of the brief, the work in all cases is the same, but at this point the debater has to decide what special preparation he shall make for handling and presenting to the audience the material that he has collected. He is puzzled to know whether it will be worth while to expand his brief; and if he does expand it, he is in doubt as to just what he should do with the expanded argument.

A debater has his choice of several possible methods of procedure. The simplest, though not the most effective method, is to write out the argument in full, and to memorize it word for word. The weakness of such a course lies in the immobility of its attack and defense. The first speaker for the affirmative may decide beforehand exactly what he will say and the order in which he will say it, but all those who are to follow should adapt their arguments, to some extent at least, to the exigencies of the debate. They will find it desirable to make a change in one place in order to join their arguments harmoniously to those of their colleagues; they will wish to make changes in another place for the sake of assailing an obviously weak spot or in order to ward off an unexpected attack. This versatility is practically impossible if one is delivering an argument that he has memorized word for word. Again, a memorized argument cannot carry with it the force and the conviction that may be found in an effort of a more spontaneous character. Furthermore, if a debater should be so unfortunate as to forget even a few words of a memorized selection, he would probably be forced to sit down with his speech only partially completed.

Another method that some debaters follow is to memorize portions of their argument and to extemporize the rest. This is open to two great objections: first, it is difficult to join together gracefully the memorized passages and the extempo-

Debate

rized; and the second, the very smoothness with which the memorized passages are delivered betrays the crudeness and awkwardness of the extemporized parts.

A third method, and undoubtedly the best one for the student to adopt, is not to expand the brief before he debates, but to memorize the greater part of it *as a brief*. In this way a debater has his ideas well in hand, and, without being tied down to any particular manner of expression or obliged to follow any set order of procedure, he can use his material as opportunity requires. His language should be at least partially extemporaneous; he may have a fairly clear conception of how he is to frame his sentences, but he should have nothing learned word for word. Thus his speech may have an element of spontaneity that will give it a tone of sincerity and earnestness unattainable when one is repeating a memorized passage. Too much, however, must not be left to the inspiration of the moment; no student should ever try to debate without first attempting in his room to expand his brief orally. He is sure to meet with considerable difficulty the first time he tries to formulate his ideas in clear, forceful, and elegant language; but several attempts will produce a remarkable change. After

253

Debate

a few endeavors he will discover ways of expressing himself that he will remember, even though the words vary greatly each time.

The superiority of this method is marked. It enables the debater to become perfectly familiar with all his material, and it gives him a fairly good idea of what language he shall use. He is not, however, bound down to any set speech; he can alter his argument to suit the occasion. Should he unexpectedly find that his opponent has admitted a certain idea, he can merely call attention to this fact and not waste valuable time in giving superfluous proof. If he sees that his opponent has made such a strong argument that some refutation is necessary at the outset in order to gain the confidence of his audience, he can instantly change the order of his proof and begin with a point that he had, perhaps, intended to use in another part of his speech. In fact, this method enables one to *debate* rather than to *declaim*.

In most debating contests it is permissible for the contestants to make use of a few notes written on small cards that can be carried in a pocket or held unobtrusively in the hand. Such a practice, if not abused, is commended by some teachers of argumentation. On these cards the debater can put down the main headings of his brief, all statistics that are difficult to remember, and all quotations. *He had better not refer to these cards for the headings of his brief if he can possibly avoid doing so.* It will be a great stimulus, however, for him to know that he has this help to rely on in case of necessity. Statistics and quotations he may read without hesitation.

One should speak his debate many times by himself, not only for the purpose of gaining facility in expression, but also for the sake of condensing his material to an argument that will approximately occupy the exact time allowed him for debating. It is a deplorable fact that many debaters try to say so much that when their allotment of time has expired they find themselves in the very midst of their argument. Such an ending leaves the audience confused and unimpressed. No debater should ever omit his conclusion. If there is only one contestant on each side, a conclusion is certainly necessary both for the sake of clearness and emphasis, and because an unfinished argument is not a unit. If there are several contestants on each side, the fact that the opposing speakers intervene and distract the attention of the audience makes it even more necessary that each debater end his argument with a formal conclusion, and by means of it bind his work to that of his colleagues.

REFUTATION.

As much time, if not more, should be spent in preparing the destructive as in preparing the constructive portion of an argument. One can determine beforehand almost exactly how he will establish his side of the proposition, but just what material he will need to overthrow his opponent's proof will depend upon how that proof is constructed. Ordinarily one can predict what lines of reasoning an opponent will take; in fact, no one should ever attempt to debate until he has studied the proposition so thoroughly that he can anticipate practically all the arguments that will be advanced. Yet until he sees on what points the emphasis is placed, what arguments are ignored, and what evidence is used, he cannot tell for sure what facts and what inferences will be most valuable as refutation. Therefore, a debater who wishes to offer good refutation must have a wealth of material at his command and be able to select instantly the ideas that will be of the greatest value.

Debate

This necessity for an abundance of information precludes the idea, held by some, that good debaters depend for their refutation on the inspiration of the moment. Great speakers often spend incalculable time in preparing to answer the arguments of the opposition. Webster's *Reply to Hayne,* which is a recognized masterpiece of oratory, and which is almost entirely refutation, was at first thought to have been composed over night, but Webster declared that all the material he had used had lain in his desk for months.

Refutation should come for the most part, though not entirely, in the rebuttal. Unless one has made a thorough study of both sides of the question, and is thus sure of his ground, anticipatory refutation is dangerous. It is sometimes an excellent plan to take the wind out of an opponent's sails by over-throwing an argument of his before he has a chance to present it, but in doing this the debater must use the greatest caution. To begin with, he must be sure that the argument he refutes is of such a fundamental nature that it is essential to the case of the other side, for if his opponent fails to use this point, the debater not only has exposed himself to ridicule, but has wasted valuable time. When one does refute in advance a point that must be up-

Debate

held by the opposition, a skillful opponent often can, by calling attention to the fact that even those on the other side recognize the importance and strength of this argument, destroy much of the advantage that has been gained. To refute an argument before it is advanced, sometimes brings failure and sometimes brings success. A debater must exercise judgment.

One must also exercise a high degree of judgment in deciding where he can most advantageously answer the arguments that have actually been given. Whenever a debater presents so thorough and so strong proof that the audience is likely to think that he has settled the question and won the debate, the succeeding speaker on the opposite side will have great difficulty in making any impression unless he can at the start at least partially discredit the preceding argument. The attitude of the audience will compel him to use refutation before beginning his constructive work. On the other hand, if the preceding argument has apparently produced but little effect, he may at once begin to build his own proof. He should, however, show good reason for postponing his refutation. To ignore the previous arguments entirely, or arbitrarily to postpone answering them, is likely to give the audience an unfavorable impression.

Common errors in refutation. A common error in refutation is the failure to attack an opponent's main arguments. Students especially are wont to neglect fundamental principles, and instead of overthrowing the points that count, occupy invaluable time with trivial matters. To rebut unimportant details, admitted matter, mere illustrations, and errors obviously due to haste in speaking, is a fault that every debater should carefully avoid. Such trivialities the audience immediately forgets, and to bring them up again and refute them serves no worthy purpose whatever.

Another serious fault common to refutation in student debates is lack of coherence. The student falls into this error when he rebuts a miscellaneous lot of points without having first ascertained the function of each and differentiated the main ideas from the subordinate ones. Instead of looking at the argument as a whole and attacking it with the concerted strength of all his forces, he fires scattering shots, and does but little damage. In refutation a debater must first see clearly the relation between each point that he rebuts and the proposition, otherwise his work is wasted. Secondly, he must make this relation perfectly plain to the audience. Instead of overthrowing isolated statements, a debater should take up his opponent's case as *a whole* and weaken it as much as he can. He should attack each main point. Coherent refutation adds much to the effectiveness of a debate.

Availability of material for refutation. In offering refutation, every inexperienced debater has difficulty in laying his hands on just the material that he desires to use. Possibly he remembers that he has seen somewhere an article that proves the insincerity of a man who has just been quoted as an authority; but if he can neither produce this article nor state its substance, he might as well not know about it. Perhaps he remembers having seen a table of statistics showing that his opponent has erred in regard to the death rate in the Spanish-American War; but unless he can produce the table, his knowledge is of no avail. There is scarcely any time for searching through books or unorganized notes; material to be of use must be instantly available. Some definite system of arranging rebuttal material is absolutely indispensable.

One method that has been tried with great success consists of putting down on cards of a uniform

Debate

size all the material that can possibly be of use in refutation. These cards the debater then groups, in alphabetical order, under headings that correspond to the main divisions of the subject under discussion, and if it seems advisable in any particular instance, he may group them under subdivisions of the proposition. To be more explicit, if a debater thinks that the opposition may question the financial success of a plan that he is advocating, he should write out on as many cards as are necessary, usually putting only one idea on each card, all the material that goes to show why the plan should succeed and where it has succeeded. Furthermore, if the plan has failed anywhere, he should put down, providing he is able, explanations that will account for the failure without condemning the system. These cards, then, would naturally be arranged under some such heading as " Finance " or " Success." If the debater wishes, he may also arrange his cards under subheadings. For instance, those cards that go to show why the plan ought to succeed could be put under the subheading, " Antecedent Probability "; those that show where the plan has succeeded, under " Sign," and those that account for failure of the plan in certain places, under the heading " Failures." Any one at all famil-

Debate

iar with a library card catalogue will at once see the various possibilities for arranging these cards.

Cards for rebuttal should be made out about as follows :—

Proposition :— *Resolved,* That profit-sharing and co-operative methods generally afford the most promising solution of the labor problem. (Affirmative.)

PRACTICABILITY

Practicability

The Union Polishing Metal Plating Company has been successfully operated under this method since 1902. (C. H. Quinn, Outlook, Vol. LXXIII, page 452.)

Debate

Practicability

The great iron works of Evansville, Wis., are operated under this method. (G. L. McNutt, Ind., Vol. LV, page 619.)

The advantages of such a system are obvious. This method gives not only one debater, but the whole team, almost instant command of all the material that has been collected. One can find what he wants, and find it hastily; he is not obliged to spend much valuable time in hunting after needed evidence and thus neglect large portions of the speech that is being delivered. A debater should begin on the classification of rebuttal material almost as soon as he begins to read on his subject. In this way he will save all the material that he gathers, and his catalogued information will be of assistance to him in drawing his brief and in constructing his main argument as well as in making refutation at the time of the debate.

WHAT EACH DEBATER MUST DO.

The first speaker for the affirmative. Upon the first speaker for the affirmative falls the duty of interpreting the proposition. Since the subject of analysis has already been fully discussed, but few directions need be given here. It may be well, however, to emphasize the qualities of clearness and fairness. A debate, unlike a written argument, cannot be studied and re-read time and again. For this reason, unless the proposition is explained in the very simplest language and by means of the very clearest definitions and illustrations, many people in the audience will not understand what the debate is about. Long words and high-sounding phrases have no place here. The debater must aim to reach not merely those who are familiar with the subject, but also those to whom the question is absolutely new. If, when the first speaker has finished, any attentive listener of average intelligence fails to understand both the subject of the debate and the attitude of the affirmative side, the speech has been a failure.

Then, too, the analysis of the proposition must be fair and just to both sides. A debater has no right to strain or twist the meaning of the proposition so as to gain any advantage for himself. In the first place, this practice is dishonest, and an honorable debater does not wish to win by trickery or fraud. Secondly, such an act almost always brings defeat. The fact that a debate is being held, presupposes a subject about which reasonable men may differ. If a debater interprets the proposition so that only one reasonable side exists, manifestly he must be in error, and upon the exposure of this error he is sure to lose the decision.

In debate, therefore, clearness and fairness should especially characterize the four steps that are taken in analyzing the proposition: to define terms, to explain the proposition as a whole, to discover the issues, and to make the partition.

Upon the completion of the introduction, the first debater for the affirmative proceeds to the discussion, and later, should he be the only contestant on the affirmative side, to the conclusion. But if, as is usually the case, there be several debaters on each side, he takes up only one or two main points of the proof. In handling this proof he must be sure so to correlate his work with the work of his colleagues that, in the minds of the audience, it will all hang together as a united whole. To accomplish this object, he may, as he finishes with his partition, state what points he will discuss himself, and what points will be handled by the affirmative speakers that are to succeed him; and he must, without fail, when he nears the end of his allotted time, hastily summarize the proof that he has given, and outline the proof that is to follow. In this way he may keep the intervening speeches of his opponents from entirely destroying the continuity that should exist between his speech and the speeches of his colleagues.

The first speaker for the negative. It rests with the first speaker for the negative to determine whether the introduction as presented by the affirmative is satisfactory, whether the analysis of the proposition is clear, adequate, and fair. If the affirmative has erred in any respect, it is the duty of the first negative debater to supply the deficiency or make the correction; otherwise he errs equally with the affirmative. If the affirmative has failed to explain the proposition so that it is generally understood, the negative is sure to win favor with the audience by spending a few moments in elucidating the subject of controversy. If the affirmative debater has analyzed the question inadequately or unfairly, the negative debater should not begin to establish proof until he has set these preliminaries straight. In correcting an unfair analysis, it is never enough that one merely make objections or even give an introduction of his own; he must, in brief form — and often a single sentence is sufficient — show to the satisfaction of the audience that his opponent has not interpreted the proposition correctly. On the other hand, if the first speaker for the negative considers the introduction given by the affirmative perfectly fair and satisfactory, he can pass by it without comment, and begin his own argument either with refutation or with a statement of the points that the negative side will establish in attacking the proposition.

It is thus apparent that a debater who opens a negative argument must depend for the beginning of his speech rather on a thorough understanding of the subject in all its details and fundamental principles than on a speech that he has to deliver word for word. To repeat an introduction that has already been given is absurd; to fail to correct an introduction that, as a whole, is obscure or is unfair, is to merit defeat. It may be added, by way of caution, that when a debater supplies any deficiencies in the speech of his predecessor, he should do this without any appearance of " smartness " or personal antagonism. Even if the affirmative debater has been manifestly unfair, the negative speaker will do well to correct this unfairness in a friendly, though in a forceful manner.

As soon as the introduction is out of the way,

the negative speaker proceeds to the discussion. Two courses are open to him: he may at once refute his predecessor's arguments, or he may proceed to take up his constructive proof, giving reason for postponing the refutation. As this matter has already been discussed, it is only necessary to say that the course he should choose depends largely upon the strength of the preceding argument. The same directions that have been given to the affirmative debater for connecting his work to his colleagues' apply equally to the negative. Summaries and outlines aid greatly in binding the arguments of a debating team into one compact mass.

The other speakers. About the only practical suggestion which can be made to the other speakers is that they adapt their constructive work to that of their colleagues, and deploy their refutation so as to hammer the principal positions of their opponents. Each debater may or may not begin his speech with refutation, but he should always begin his main argument with a terse, clear summary of what has been said on his side, and in closing he should not only summarize his own arguments, but he should also give again, in very brief form, the gist of what has been proved by his colleagues. In addition, any speaker except the last one on each side, may, if he thinks best, give an outline of the argument to follow. In making these summaries, a debater must always avoid stating them in so bald and crude a form as to make them monotonous and offensive. He ought rather to use all the ingenuity at his command in an attempt to make this repetition exceedingly forceful.

It often happens that an inexperienced debater never reaches his conclusion. While he is still in the midst of his proof, his allotment of time expires, and he is forced to sit down, leaving his speech hanging in the air. Such an experience is both awkward and disastrous; a skillful debater never allows it to happen. The peroration is the most important part of an argument, and on it the debater should lavish his greatest care. To omit it is almost the same as to have made no speech at all. As soon as the debater perceives that he has but a short time left, he should at once bring this main speech to a close, and even though he may have to omit important ideas, begin at once on his conclusion. As is pointed out in Chapter X, the conclusion consists both of a summary and an emotional appeal. What emotion shall be aroused and how it shall apply to the summarized headings can largely be determined beforehand. Some debaters go so far

Debate

as to commit this conclusion to memory. This practice is not recommended except in special cases, and yet a debater should be so familiar with his peroration that he will have no difficulty in putting it into vigorous and pleasing language.

Rebuttal speeches. A rebuttal speech usually furnishes an excellent test of a debater's mastery of his subject. It shows whether or not he comprehends the fundamental principles that underly the argument. If he does not understand fundamentals, he cannot distinguish between what is worth answering and what is trivial. If he is not perfectly familiar with the arguments on both sides of the question, his refutation will be scattering; that is, he will rebut only a few of his opponent's headings, those for which, in his scanty preparation, he has discovered some answer. On the other hand, if he really understands the subject, he will deal largely with main ideas; and if his knowledge of the subject is as extensive as it should be, he will almost invariably be able to offer some opposition to every main heading used by the opposition.

When a debate is held between only two contestants, each one has to refute the whole argument of his opponent. In this case there are no complications; but when two teams are debating, the mem-

Debate

bers of each must decide among themselves as to how the rebuttal shall be handled. One way is for each member to refute all he can, working independently of his colleagues. Much better results are secured, however, when a team works systematically. In the first place, a team should always resolve the opposing arguments into a hasty brief. The main points of the opposition can then be assigned for rebuttal to the various members of the team, and each debater can give thorough treatment to his assignment. In this way every point is sure to be covered, and there will be little, if any, duplication of work.

Such a course presupposes very careful preparation on the part of the debaters. It means that each member of the team must have sufficient knowledge and material at his command to oppose with credit any argument that may be advanced. In general, the assignment of headings for rebuttal may be such that each debater will refute those points of which he took an opposite view in his main speech, but as it is usually desirable to rebut arguments in the same order in which they were originally given, no member of the team can afford to shirk mastering each detail that in any way has a vital bearing upon the proposition.

Debate

The last rebuttal speaker. The work of the last speaker on each side differs somewhat from the work of his colleagues. All the speakers try to overthrow the opposing arguments, and by means of summaries keep their case as a whole before the audience. The last speaker devotes far less time to pure refutation, gives a more detailed summary, and, in addition, compares and contrasts the arguments of his side with the arguments of the opposition. This last process is called " amplifying and diminishing."

It is not always necessary to prove a main heading false in order to destroy its effectiveness. A debater may of necessity have to admit that the opposition has successfully established the points it set out to prove. In such a case, he cannot do better than to acknowledge the correctness of his opponent's proof, and then remembering that an audience awards a decision by a comparison of the relative weight of the proof of each side, amplify the importance of his own arguments, point by point, and diminish the importance of the arguments advanced by the other side.

For instance, in a debate on the question as to whether immigration should be restricted, the affirmative might maintain that unrestricted immigration brings serious political evils, and the negative might show that the policy of nonrestriction greatly increases the wealth of the country. If neither of these contentions be successfully refuted, the favor of the audience will incline towards the affirmative or the negative, as far as those two points are concerned, according as they think that political purity or economic prosperity is the more important. Plainly, it would be for the interest of the affirmative to convince the audience that the preservation of political integrity is of greater moment than any mere material gain.

In many respects the last rebuttal speeches on each side are the most conspicuous and decisive parts of a debate. If the last speech is hesitating and weak, it is liable to ruin all preceding efforts, even though they were of the highest order; if it is enthusiastic and strong, it will often cover up preceding defects, and turn defeat into victory. Because of its importance this portion of the work usually falls to the best debater on the team, and if he is wise he will give it his greatest thought and care. In this speech he should strive in every possible way to attain perfection. His delivery should be emphatic and pleasing; his ideas should be logically arranged; and his knowledge of what he has to say should be so complete that there will be no hesitation, no groping for words. Furthermore, he should introduce an element of persuasion; to reach both the minds and the hearts of his hearers is essential for the greatest success. All this has to be done in a short time, yet to be of a high rank even the shortest closing speeches must contain these characteristics.

SPECIAL FEATURES OF DEBATE.

An argument, like other kinds of composition, should possess the qualities of style known as Clearness, Force, and Elegance, and should in all respects observe the principles of Unity, Selection, Coherence, Proportion, Emphasis, and Variety. Since the student from his study of Rhetoric is already familiar with these matters, it would be superfluous to dwell upon them in this book. A good written argument, however, does not always make a good debate; limited time for speaking, lack of opportunity for the audience to grasp ideas and to reflect upon them, the presence of strong opposing arguments that must be met and overthrown with still stronger arguments,— these conditions render the

Debate

heightening of certain characteristics indispensable in a debate.

Above all else the successful debater is forceful. He uses every possible device for driving home his arguments. He bends every effort toward making his ideas so plain and so emphatic that the audience will understand them and *remember* them. Realizing that the audience cannot, like the reader of a written article, peruse the argument a second time, he uses words and expressions that cause his thoughts to stick fast wherever they fall.

Statistics. Statistics improperly used are dry and uninteresting; they often spoil an otherwise forceful and persuasive debate. The trouble often lies, strange to say, in the accuracy with which the figures are given. A brain that is already doing its utmost to accept almost instantaneously a multitude of facts and comprehend their significance, or a brain that is somewhat sluggish and lazy, refuses to be burdened with uninteresting and unimportant details. For this reason, when a debater speaks of 10,564,792 people, the brain becomes wearied with the numbers and in disgust is apt to turn away from the whole matter. On the other hand, the round sum 10,000,000 not only does not burden the brain, but also, under ordinary conditions, gives in a rather forceful manner the information it was intended to convey. " About five hundred " presents a much more vivid picture than " four hundred and eighty-six " or " five hundred and eighteen "; " fifteen per cent." is stronger than " fifteen and one-tenth per cent."; the expression " eighty years " seems to indicate a longer period of time than " eighty-two years, seven months, and twenty-nine days."

If one is to quote statistics, he should always, unless the circumstances be very unusual, use round numbers. Figures themselves, however, are often less emphatic than other methods of expression. The ordinary mind can not grasp the significance of large numbers. That the state of Texas contains over a quarter of a million of square miles means little to the average person; he neither remembers the exact area of other states nor can he realize what an immense territory these figures stand for. The following quotation gives the area of Texas in much more vivid and forceful language :—

If you take Texas by the upper corner and swing it on that as a pivot, you will lop off the lower end of California, cut through Idaho, overlap South Dakota, touch Michigan, bisect Ohio, reach West Virginia, cut through North Carolina and South Carolina, lop off all the western side of Florida, and blanket the greater part of the Gulf of Mexico.

To say that the American farmer produced in 1907 a crop worth, at the farm, seven and one-half billions of dollars, conveys little idea of the magnitude of the harvest. A current magazine has couched the same estimate in less exact but in far more emphatic language:—

Suppose that all of last year's corn had been shipped to Europe; it would have required over four thousand express steamers of 18,000 tons register to deliver it. Suppose that the year's wheat had all been sent to save the Far East from a great famine: the largest fleet in the world, with its four hundred vessels of all sizes, would have required fifteen round trips to move it. Take to-bacco,— such a minor crop that most people never think of it in connection with farming:— if last year's tobacco crop had been made into cigars, the supply would have lasted 153,000 men for fifty years, each man smoking ten cigars a day.

The officials of the forestry service, in speaking of the great devastation caused by forest fires, make the startling assertion that a new navy of first-class battle-ships could be built for the sum lost during a few weeks in the fires that raged from the pines of Maine to the redwoods of California.

Figures used in this way are most effective, and yet probably nothing in argumentation is more tedious than too many of these descriptions of statistics coming close together. If numbers absolutely have to be indicated a great many times, even figures are likely to be less tiresome.

Concreteness. General statements and abstract principles invariably weary an audience. Theories and generalities are usually too intangible to make much impression. Specific instances and concrete cases, however, are usually interesting. A vivid picture of real persons, things, and events is necessary to arouse the attention of an audience and cause them both to understand the argument and to give it their consideration. The slogan of a recent political campaign was not, " Improved economic conditions for the laboring man "; it was, " The full dinner pail." The political orator who is urging the necessity for a larger navy on the ground that war is imminent does not speak of possible antagonists in such general terms as *foreign powers;* he specifies Germany, Japan, and the other nations that he fears. The preacher who would really awaken the conscience of his church does not confine himself to such terms as *original sin* and *weaknesses of the flesh;* he talks of *lying, stealing,* and *swearing.*

Compare the effectiveness of the following examples :—

Debate

People of the same race are more loyal to each other than to foreigners.

Blood is thicker than water.

Western farmers are demanding political recognition.

" No, I am not going to vote a straight ticket this year. If I do, my candidate must be in favor of some things I want." That was the dictum of Franklin Taylor, Farmer, on Rural Route No. 12, ten miles from a western town. He is a type of thousands of other farmers in the West.

Business streets that were once commodious and impressive are now smoky and filthy.

Business streets that ten years after the great fire promised to be almost grand in their width and perspective are now mere smoky tunnels under the filth-dripping gridirons of the elevated railways.

Debate

The West is becoming more densely populated.	The center of population, now in Indiana, is traveling straight toward the middle point of Illinois. The center of manufacturing has reached only eastern Ohio, but is marching in a bee-line for Chicago.

In the following quotation Mr. Crisp, laying aside for the moment abstractions and generalities, and bringing his case down to a specific instance, gives a concrete illustration of how the protective tariff affects a single individual:

Will you tell how this protective tariff benefits our agricultural producers? I can show you — I think I can demonstrate clearly — how the tariff hurts them; and I defy any of you to show wherein they are benefited by a protective tariff.

Suppose a farmer in Minnesota has 5,000 bushels of wheat and a farmer in Georgia has 100 bales of cotton. That wheat at eighty cents a bushel is worth $4,000, and that cotton at eight cents a pound is worth $4,000. Let those producers ship their staples abroad. The Minnesota wheat-grower ships his wheat to Liverpool; whether he ships it there or not, that is where the price of his wheat is fixed. The Georgia cotton-raiser ships his cotton to Liverpool; whether he ships it there or not, that is where the price of his cotton is fixed. The wheat and the cotton are sold in that free trade market. The wheat is sold for $4,000; the cotton brings the same amount. The Minnesota farmer invests the $4,000 he has received for his wheat in clothing, crockery, iron, steel, dress goods, clothing,— whatever he may need for his family in Minnesota. The Georgia cotton-raiser invests the proceeds of his cotton in like kind of goods.

Each of those men ships his goods to this country and they reach the port of New York. When either undertakes to unload them he is met by the collector of customs, who says, "Let me see your invoice." The invoice is exhibited, and it shows $4,000 worth of goods. Those goods represent in the one case 5,000 bushels of wheat, in the other case 100 bales of cotton. The collector at the port says to either of these gentlemen — the man who raises the wheat in Minnesota or him who raises the cotton in Georgia, "You cannot bring into this market those goods for which you have exchanged your products unless you pay to the United States a tariff by the McKinley law — a tax of $2,000."

Figures of speech. The use of figurative language is also an aid to clearness and to force. Simile, metaphor, personification, antithesis, balance, climax, rhetorical question, and repetition are all effective aids in the presentation of argument. The speeches of great orators are replete with expressions of this sort. Burke, in his *Speech on Conciliation,* says, "Despotism itself is obliged to truck and huckster"; "The public," he said, "would not have patience to see us play the game out with our adversaries; we must produce our hand"; "Men may lose little in property by the act which takes away

281

Debate

all their freedom. When a man is robbed of a trifle on the highway, it is not the twopence lost that constitutes the capital outrage." In speaking of certain provisions of the Constitution, Webster says that they are the " keystone of the arch." The following paragraph is taken from his *Reply to Hayne:*—

And, sir, where American liberty raised its first voice, and where its youth was nurtured and sustained, there it still lives in the strength of its manhood and full of its original spirit. If discord and disunion shall wound it; if party strife and blind ambition shall hawk at and tear it; if folly and madness, if uneasiness under salutary and necessary restraint, shall succeed to separate it from that Union by which alone its existence is made sure; it will stand, in the end, by the side of that cradle in which its infancy was rocked; it will stretch forth its arm with whatever of vigor it may still retain, over the friends who gather round it; and it will fall at last, if fall it must, amidst the proudest monuments of its own glory, and on the very spot of its origin.

The Outlook, in a recent issue, first states a vital question in literal and then, to drive home the meaning of the problem, in figurative language:—

Is the Constitution of the United States a series of inflexible rules which can be changed only by the methods which those rules themselves prescribe, or is it the expression of certain political principles by which a living and growing Nation has resolved to guide itself in its life and growth? Is it an anchor which fastens the ship of state in one place, or a rudder to guide it on its voyage?

Sometimes figures of speech are used to such excess or in such incongruous combinations that they detract from the effectiveness of the debate in which they occur rather than add to it. The distance from a forceful figure to an absurd figure is so short that a debater has to be on his guard against using expressions that will impress his audience as ridiculous or even funny. A mixture of highly figurative language with literal language and commonplace ideas, and a mixture of several figures are especially to be guarded against. As an example of the extent to which figures may be mixed the following will serve:—

"I'm up a tree," admitted the bolting Senator, "but my back is to the wall and I'll die in the last ditch, going down with flags flying, and from the mountain top of Democracy, hurling defiance at the foe, soar on the wings of triumph, regardless of the party lash that barks at my heels."

DELIVERY.

To be a successful debater one must understand how to talk and how to act in the presence of an audience. Uncouthness in appearance and awk-

Debate

wardness in speech have often brought defeat. Moreover, it is not enough that a debater refrain from offending his audience; his bearing and his voice should be of positive assistance to him both in pleasing them and in interpreting to them the ideas that he wishes to convey. First of all, a good delivery is one that assists in making the argument clear. Its next most important function is to make the argument forceful. A speaker should never rest content with being able to present his argument merely with clearness; he should strive to be interesting and impressive also. These qualities depend in no small measure upon the way a speech is delivered. The best story or the best argument will fall flat unless it is full of the fire of enthusiasm, unless the personality of the speaker vivifies it and makes it a living reality. Unfortunately, this intangible quality in a speaker, often called " personality " or " magnetism," cannot, to any great extent, be taught. In the main, one must seek this and develop it for himself. A text-book can point out what constitutes good form, what is pleasing and impressive to the eye and to the ear, and, in a word, what make up the externals of a good delivery; but beyond these mechanical directions it cannot go. A student should observe the follow-

Debate

ing fundamental directions as his first step toward becoming a successful speaker. Afterwards, he should cultivate earnestness, enthusiasm, perception, a sense of humor, and all other such qualities as go to make up a really great speaker.

Position. The best position for a debater to take on the stage is in the centre well toward the front. He should take the centre because in that position he can best see the entire audience, and the entire audience can best see him. He should stand near the front edge of the platform for several reasons: first, he can make himself more easily understood; his voice need not be so loud in order to be heard distinctly in every part of the hall. This is no small advantage for one who is not gifted with unusual powers of speech. In the next place, if a debater stands close to his audience, he can adopt a more conversational style of delivery. He can establish a direct personal connection between himself and his hearers and talk to them as man to man. If the hall is not too large, he need scarcely raise his voice from its accustomed tone; he can look his audience in the eye, receiving the stimulus of whatever interest they express; and at the same time he can let them see in his features the earnestness and sincerity that he feels. To stand near the back of the stage is undoubtedly easier for one who is diffident or inexperienced; perhaps he will then be able partially to forget where he is and to imagine that he is alone; but such an attitude both severs all personal connection between speaker and hearer, and shows that the debater does not trust himself, that he has no great belief in his subject, and that he fears his audience. An impression of this sort is a great handicap even to the strongest case. If one would inspire confidence, he must appear confident; if one would make friends, he must be friendly, avoiding even a suggestion of aloofness. To accomplish these purposes as far as is possible by *action,* a debater should come close to his audience, having every appearance of being glad that he is to speak and confident in the strength of the side that he is to uphold.

The next thing for a speaker to learn is how to stand. He should not take a natural posture, as some writers say, unless that posture is one of strength and, to some degree, of grace. A student without training will usually stand with his head protruding forward, his shoulders drooping, his body twisted, and his feet far apart, with all his weight on one leg. Such an attitude is enough to condemn one even before he begins to speak. A

Debate

slipshod appearance suggests slipshod thinking and reasoning. A speaker should always stand erect, with his head back, chin in, shoulders rolled back and down; either the feet should be near together with the weight of the body on both, or one foot should be slightly in advance of the other with the weight of the body entirely on the rear foot. In the latter case, the leg on which the body rests must form a straight line with the body, there being no unsightly bulging at the hip; and the leg on which the body does not rest must be slightly bent at the knee. This posture is not difficult to attain if one will practise it frequently, endeavoring in his everyday life to walk and stand in a soldierly manner. On the other hand, erectness should not be carried to such an extreme as to become stiffness. A debater's object is to be forceful and pleasing. In striving for this end, he should always remember that he can very easily err in either of two directions.

A debater should allow his hands, for the most part, to hang naturally at his sides. There may be a great temptation for him to put them in his pockets, but he should resist this for two reasons: such a procedure is not considered good form, and his hands are less available for instant use in the making of gestures. If one is delivering a lengthy argument, there is no particular harm in putting one hand behind the back for a short time, or even in front of the body along the waist line, provided this can be done in an easy, natural manner; but in the case of a short speech, one will do well to keep his hands at his sides. They must hang naturally in order not to attract attention, being neither closed tightly nor held rigidly open. If one will follow these directions, his hands and arms may feel awkward, but they will not appear so.

Another important principle in the matter of position requires that a debater shall keep his eyes fixed on his audience. He must not look at the floor, at the ceiling, or at the walls. He must look at the people he would convince. Only in this way can he hope to hold their attention. Only in this way can he win their confidence and reach their feelings. To look into space means to debate into space.

In the next place, a speaker must beware of falling into ludicrous and disgusting habits of deportment. Nervousness will often cause one in the presence of an audience to keep making an unsightly gesture, a peculiar twitch or step that will absolutely ruin his whole speech. Some speakers have been known to change their weight from one

Debate

foot to the other as often as twenty or thirty times a minute. Other speakers have adopted a peculiar jerk of the head or a constant shrugging of the shoulders that is most disagreeable to see. Still others keep constantly opening and shutting their hands. For years one speaker of some small prominence spent the greater part of his time while on the platform in tugging at his coat, apparently in an effort to make it fit better around the collar. All such actions as these are to be carefully guarded against.

A debater, however, is not expected to stand perfectly still: he should use considerable interpretative and emphatic action. To begin with, he ought not to stand all the time in exactly the same spot. Monotony of position is to be avoided as well as monotony of action or of voice. He will rest himself and his audience if he will occasionally move about, taking two or three steps at a time. In doing this he must never go backward; he must never retreat. If, for any reason, he began his speech while standing near the rear or the centre of the stage, he should move forward; if he cannot go forward, he may move back and forth near the edge of the platform. The best time for one to change his position is at the conclusion of a paragraph.

Debate

A paragraph division, it will be remembered, indicates a change in thought. If a debater, therefore, makes a longer pause than usual at this point, and in addition alters his position slightly, he helps interpret his argument. He does for the hearer exactly what indentation does for the reader.

Gestures. So much has been said and written about gestures that a student is often puzzled to know whose advice to follow and what to do. Some writers say that no gestures at all are desirable; others deem them necessary, but declare that they should never be made unless they are spontaneous and natural. In the light of such conflicting advice, what will determine the proper course for a student to follow? The answer to this question lies in a consideration of the ultimate object of a course in debating. If it is to give students some facility in expressing their thoughts before an audience, if it is to train students for practical work in business and professional life, then those men who are recognized as the polished and powerful speakers of the day should be taken as models. Most of these, it will be found, use gestures. There is but one reasonable course, then, for the student to follow: he should make gestures. They may be crude and awkward at first, but only by practice can he ever hope to improve them.

The best method of procedure, undoubtedly, is for the beginner to become familiar with two or three of the most common gestures, learning how to make them and just what they signify. He should then use them. They may seem mechanical and ungainly at first, but constant practice both in private and before a class will soon enable him to make them with considerable emphasis and ease. From this point on, the road is clear. The knowledge that he can use his hands to good advantage, even in a limited way, will soon cause him to make gestures spontaneously. Nor will he be limited to the few with which he started. In the midst of an explanation and in the heat of an impassioned plea, he will find himself using gestures that he had not thought of before. The awkward and premeditated gesture with which he began will have become forceful and spontaneous.

The gestures that a student should first learn to use must be illustrated to him by his instructor. To see a gesture made several times gives one a better idea of how to make it and of what it means than could a dozen pages in a text-book. The choice of gestures, too, may rest with the instructor. It makes no particular difference with what ones a debater begins, provided that they are simple in execution and are such as he will wish to use in practically every debate into which he enters. Ordinarily, the best ones for a beginner to practice on are those indicating emphasis. If he wishes for a wider field, he might also try to use gestures indicating magnitude and contrast. When he has finished with these, he should hesitate before deliberately introducing many others. A debate is not a dramatic production, and it should in no wise savor of melodrama.

Voice. Correct position and forceful gestures are very important, but upon no one thing does the success of a debater, aside from his argument, depend so much as upon his voice. One may move his audience in spite of an awkward posture and in the absence of all intelligent gestures, but unless his voice meets certain requirements, his case is almost hopeless. Above all else a speaker's voice must be distinct.

Distinctness depends upon several things. First, the voice must be loud enough to be heard without difficulty in every part of the room. To produce this result, one should speak especially to those in the rear, carefully watching to see whether he holds their attention; at the same time he must be careful not to shout in a manner unpleasant to those sitting nearer him. The stress laid by public speakers upon the matter of loudness is well illustrated by a story told of one of the foremost orators of the day. It is said that he invariably stations some one in the back of the audience to signal to him when his voice is either too low or unnecessarily loud.

In the next place, distinctness depends upon enunciation. The debater who drops off final syllables, slurs consonants, runs words together, or talks without using his lips and without opening his mouth is hard to understand. It often requires considerable conscious effort to pronounce each syllable in a word distinctly, but the resulting clearness is worth a strenuous attempt. One great cause of poor enunciation is too rapid talking. A fairly slow delivery is preferable not only because the words can be more easily understood, but also because it gives a debater the appearance of being more careful and accurate in his reasoning. Great rapidity in speech may be due to nervousness or inexperience; whatever its cause, it is usually fatal to distinctness.

A pleasing tone of voice is not of so great moment as distinctness of utterance, yet its cultivation is by

Debate

no means to be neglected. Harsh, rasping sounds
and nasal twangs are disagreeable to hear, and no
speaker can afford to offend his audience in this
way. An unpleasant voice may be the result of
some physical defect; more often it is caused by
sheer carelessness. In most cases a little practice
will produce a wonderful change. A very common
breach of elegance in speaking is the habit of drawl-
ing out an *er* sound between words. The constant
repetition of this is exceedingly annoying. It is usually caused by an attempt to fill in a gap while the
speaker is groping about for the next word. The
best way to correct this blunder is to be so familiar
with what one is going to say that there will be no
gap to fill in; but in case one does have to hunt for
words, it is a thousand times preferable to leave the
gap unfilled. Each word should stand out by itself,
even though there is a pause of many seconds. To
offend the ears of an audience with a crude tone of
voice or with meaningless sounds is a bad violation
of propriety.

The first step to be taken in the cultivation of a
distinct and pleasing voice is to acquire the habit of
standing correctly. Under the subject of position
it was stated that the body should be kept erect, the
head thrown back, and the shoulders rolled back

and down. This posture is the best not only because it is the most graceful but because it gives the speaker the greatest command of his vocal organs. Stooping shoulders and a bowed trunk contract the lungs and diminish the supply of breath, and a bent neck renders the cords of the neck less controllable. After taking the proper position, one should next endeavor to breathe as deeply as he can. The louder he has to speak, the deeper should be his breathing. Remembering that he does not wish to talk fast, he will do well to fill his lungs at the close of each sentence, always inhaling, in order not to make an unpleasant gasping noise, through the nose. While speaking, he should control his supply of breath not by contracting the chest but by elevating the diaphragm. This procedure will give his voice a richness and a resonance that it otherwise could not have. Breathing merely from the top of the lungs means squeakiness of tone and poor control. One who breathes incorrectly will find it necessary to shout to make himself heard at a distance; one who breathes correctly can usually be heard under the same conditions by merely talking. The superiority of the round, deep tone over the shout is too obvious to need comment.

In the next place, a speaker must think about this

voice. Thought and study are as essential in the training of a voice as in the mastery of any art. A natural voice is not usually pleasing; it becomes so only through cultivation. Much of this training can be done by the speaker unaided. Few people are so insensible to qualities of sound that they cannot detect harshness and impurities even in their own utterance, provided that they will give the matter their attention. It is not enough, however, for one to watch his voice only while he is debating or while he is repeating his arguments in preparation for a debate; he must carry constant watchfulness even into his daily conversation. The services of a good instructor are invaluable, but at best they can be only auxiliary. All improvement must come through the efforts of the speaker himself.

Attitude toward opponents. If one will bear in mind that the fundamental purpose of argument — whether written or spoken — is to present truth in such a way as to influence belief, he will at once understand that a debater should always maintain toward his opponents the attitude of one who is trying to change another's belief, the attitude of friendship, fairness, and respect. Such a point of view precludes the use of satire, invective, or harsh epi-

Debate

thets. These never carry conviction; in fact, they invariably destroy the effect that an otherwise good argument might produce. Ridicule and bluster may please those who already agree with the speaker, but with these people he should be little concerned; a debater worthy of the name seeks to change the opinions of those who disagree with him. For this reason he is diplomatic, courteous, and urbane.

A debater should, moreover, keep to this same attitude even though his opponent introduce objectionable personalities. One will find it for his own best interest to do so. Good humor makes a far better impression than anger; it suggests strength and superiority, while anger, as everyone knows, is often the result of chagrin, and is used to cover up weaknesses. Besides, an audience always sympathizes with the man who is first attacked. All this does not mean that a debater should calmly submit to unfairness and vilification. On the contrary, he should defend himself spiritedly; but he should not meet abuse with abuse. To do so would be to throw away an invaluable opportunity. He should remain dignified, self-controlled, and good-humored; then by treating his opponent as one who has inadvertently fallen into error, and by pointing out the mistakes, the unfairness, and the way in which the real question has been ignored, he can gain an inestimable advantage.

The following quotations show what attitude a debater should maintain toward his opponents:—

As I do not precisely agree in opinion with any gentleman who has spoken, I shall take the liberty of detaining the committee for a few moments while I offer to their attention some observations. I am highly gratified with the temper and ability with which the discussion has hitherto been conducted. It is honorable to the House, and, I trust, will continue to be manifested on many future occasions. (Henry Clay.)

Mr. President, I had occasion a few days ago to expose the utter groundlessness of the personal charges made by the Senator from Illinois against myself and the other signers of the Independent Democratic Appeal. I now move to strike from this bill a statement which I will to-day demonstrate to be without any foundation in fact or history. I intend afterwards to move to strike out the whole clause annulling the Missouri prohibition.

I enter into this debate, Mr. President, in no spirit of personal unkindness. The issue is too grave and too momentous for the indulgence of such feelings. I see the great question before me, and that question only. (Salmon P. Chase.)

Compare the attitude of Mr. Naylor in the following quotation with the attitude of Mr. Lincoln in his debates with Senator Douglas. It is needless to point out which must have had the better effect upon the audience.

Debate

The gentleman has misconceived the spirit and tendency of Northern institutions. He is ignorant of Northern character. He has forgotten the history of his country. Preach insurrection to the Northern laborers! Preach insurrection to *me!* Who are the Northern laborers? The history of your country is their history. (Charles Naylor.)

My Fellow-Citizens: When a man hears himself somewhat misrepresented, it provokes him — at least, I find it so with myself; but when misrepresentation becomes very gross and palpable, it is more apt to amuse him. The first thing I see fit to notice is the fact that Judge Douglas alleges, after running through the history of the old Democratic and the old Whig parties, that Judge Trumbull and myself made an arrangement in 1854 by which I was to have the place of General Shields in the United States Senate, and Judge Trumbull was to have the place of Judge Douglas. Now all I have to say upon that subject is that I think no man — not even Judge Douglas — can prove it, because it is not true. I have no doubt he is "conscientious" in saying it. As to those resolutions that he took such a length of time to read, as being the platform of the Republican party in 1854, I say I never had anything to do with them, and I think Trumbull never had. (Abraham Lincoln in the Ottawa Joint Debate.)

Judge Douglas has told me that he heard my speeches north and my speeches south — that he heard me at Ottawa and at Freeport in the north, and recently at Jonesboro in the south, and that there was a very different cast of sentiment in the speeches made at the different points. I will not charge upon Judge Douglas that he willfully misrepresents me, but I call upon every fairminded man to take those speeches and read them, and I dare him to point out any difference between my speeches north and south. (Lincoln in the Charleston Joint Debate.)

Debate

HOW TO JUDGE A DEBATE.

Three judges usually award the decision in a debating contest. Their sole duty is to determine which side had the better of the argument. Sometimes the method that they shall follow in arriving at a decision is marked out for them; they are given printed slips indicating the relative importance of evidence, reasoning, delivery, and the other points that must be considered. Most commonly, however, each judge is instructed to decide for himself what constitutes excellence in debate. According to the rules governing any particular debate, the judges may cast their ballots with or without previous consultation with each other.

The following outline gives in condensed form the main points that a judge should consider. It will be of service not only to the judges of a debate but to the contestants, as it gives a comprehensive view of just what is expected of a debater.

I. Which side has the better analysis?

II. Which side has the stronger proof?

    A. Consider the preponderance of the evidence.

    B. Consider the quality of the evidence.

    C. Consider the skill used in reasoning.

Debate

III. Which side offers the better refutation?

    A. See which side has the more main points left standing after the refutation has been given.

IV. Which side has the better delivery?

    A. Consider general bearing, voice, and language.

CHAPTER X

THE CONCLUSION

MOST arguments have a more or less formal ending. Both writers and speakers, when seeking to influence the beliefs and acts of others, have usually deemed it advisable, upon completing their proof, to add a few summarizing words and to make a final appeal to the emotions. This part of the argument that comes at the close and that contains no new proof is called the *conclusion,* or the *peroration*. In spoken argument, occasionally, the conclusion is wholly ignored. If at any time, regardless of the point he may have reached, an arguer clearly perceives that he has won his case, he is wise to stop immediately and avoid the danger of adding anything that might possibly detract from his success. Such an experience may frequently happen to a salesman, a preacher, a lawyer. Arguments, however, that are written or that are delivered before large audiences cannot be curtailed in this way. Under such conditions the arguer is unable to tell

The Conclusion

when he has won his case: he must use all his proof and make it emphatic in every way possible. Therefore the student who is arguing for the sake of practice will do well to disregard exceptions and to close all his arguments, both written and spoken, with a peroration.

The same two elements — conviction and persuasion — that make up the introduction and the discussion are ordinarily found also in the conclusion. The general principles that govern the proportionate amount of each to be used in the first two divisions of an argument apply equally to the third division. In every case the relative amount of space to be devoted to conviction and to persuasion depends upon the nature of the subject and the attitude of the audience. In some instances a conclusion should consist wholly of conviction; in other instances persuasion should predominate; most commonly there should be a judicious combination of both.

In concluding an argument before the United States Supreme Court on the question of whether or not a certain law passed in New York was repugnant to the Constitution or consistent with it, Webster spoke as follows :—

To recapitulate what has been said, we maintain, first, that the Constitution, by its grants to Congress and its

303

The Conclusion

prohibitions on the States, has sought to establish one uniform standard of value, or medium of payment. Second, that, by like means, it has endeavored to provide for one uniform mode of discharging debts when they are to be discharged without payment. Third, that these objects are connected, and that the first loses much of its importance, if the last, also, be not accomplished. Fourth, that, reading the grant to Congress, and the prohibition on the States together, the inference is strong that the Constitution intended to confer exclusive power to pass bankrupt laws on Congress. Fifth, that the prohibition in the tenth section reaches to all contracts, existing or future, in the same way that the other prohibition in the same section extends to all debts existing or future. Sixth, that, upon any other construction, one great political object of the Constitution will fail of its accomplishment.[1]

In this conclusion, it will be noticed, there is no persuasion. Apparently the subject was of such a nature that only clear and logical reasoning was required. An appeal to the emotions would undoubtedly have been out of place. In direct contrast to the preceding method of summarizing a speech a good example of a persuasive conclusion may be found in *The Dartmouth College Case,* which Webster argued before this same tribunal, and which also involved the constitutionality of a State law. In this peroration Webster's emotional

[1] The Case of Ogden and Saunders. Webster's Great Speeches, page 188. Little, Brown & Co.

The Conclusion

appeal was so strong that, it is said, there was not a dry eye in the court room.

In writing as well as in speaking one must allow common sense to decide what shall be the nature of his peroration. The following is a typical example of a conclusion into which persuasion cannot well enter. It is taken from the close of a chapter, selected at random, in Darwin's *Structure and Distribution of Coral Reefs.*

It has, I think, been shown in this chapter, that subsidence explains both the normal structure and the less regular forms of those two great classes of reefs which have justly excited the astonishment of all the naturalists who have sailed through the Pacific and Indian oceans. The necessity, also, that a foundation should have existed at the proper depth for the growth of the corals over certain large areas, almost compels us to accept this theory. But further to test its truth a crowd of questions may be asked. . . . These several questions will be considered in the following chapter.

A type of conclusion far more common and usually far more effective is one that not only refers to the preceding arguments but also contains considerable persuasion. The peroration marks the final opportunity for the arguer to move his audience. Here he should make his greatest effort. Since belief and action ordinarily depend upon both

The Conclusion

the intellect and the will, the arguer who would attain success must appeal to both. Merely to call to mind the proof that he has advanced is seldom enough: he must arouse the emotions. The peroration of an argument is like the finish of a race or the last charge in a battle. In the conclusion the arguer should use his greatest skill, his strongest eloquence. Here are found the most inspiring passages in the masterpieces of oratory.

Some of the various ways for reaching the emotions have been pointed out in the chapter dealing with persuasion in the introduction. These same suggestions apply equally well to persuasion in the conclusion. The best advice that can be given, however, is for one to use his common sense. He must consider his subject, his audience, his ability, and his own interest in the case — all the circumstances in connection with his argument — and then depend, not upon some set formula, but upon his judgment to tell him in what way he can best be persuasive. The following illustrations will give some idea of how successful writers and speakers have concluded their arguments with persuasion. Notice the patriotic appeal in the first quotation:—

Whether we have or have not degenerated compared with (say) fifty or a hundred years ago may be a question

The Conclusion

difficult to settle, but it is quite clear that we are pitifully, disastrously below the normal standard of manhood and womanhood which a great nation should set itself.

Adequate nourishment for our children, immunity from exhausting and mechanical employments at the most critical period of adolescence, an extension of educational influences — can there be any objects of expenditures more likely than these to repay themselves a thousandfold in the improved vigor and intelligence which form the only sure basis of a nation's greatness?[1]

In the following the speaker points out the awful responsibility resting upon the jury and exhorts them to render justice:—

Let me, therefore, remind you, that though the day may soon come when our ashes shall be scattered before the winds of heaven, the memory of what you do cannot die. It will carry down to your posterity your honor or your shame. In the presence, and in the name of that everliving God, I do therefore conjure you to reflect that you have your characters, your consciences, that you have also the character, perhaps the ultimate destiny, of your country in your hands. In that awful name I do conjure you to have mercy upon your country and upon yourselves, and so to judge now as you will hereafter be judged; and I do now submit the fate of my client, and of that country which we have yet in common to your disposal.[2]

In the following extract from the conclusion of Webster's plea in *The Dartmouth College Case* con-

---

[1] Frances E. Warwick, Fortnightly Review, Vol. LXXIX, p. 515.
[2] John Philpot Curran, On the Liberty of the Press.

sider how he showed the magnitude of the question
that was at issue :—

The case before the court is not of ordinary importance,
nor of everyday occurrence. It affects not this college
only, but every college, and all the literary institutions of
the country. They have flourished hitherto, and have become in a high degree respectable and useful to the community. They have all a common principle of existence,
the inviolability of their charters. It will be a dangerous,
a most dangerous experiment, to hold these institutions
subject to the rise and fall of popular parties, and the
fluctuation of political opinions. If the franchise may at
any time be taken away, or impaired, the property also
may be taken away, or impaired, or its use perverted.
Benefactors will have no certainty of effecting the object
of their bounty; and learned men will be deterred from
devoting themselves to the service of such institutions,
from the precarious title of their offices. Colleges and
halls will be deserted by all better spirits, and become a
theatre for the contentions of politics. Party and faction
will be cherished in the places consecrated to piety and
learning. These consequences are neither remote nor possible only. They are certain and immediate.[1]

As a rule, most of the criticisms that can be
made of any conclusion pertain to matters of taste
and judgment. A writer or speaker may have
made too detailed or too brief a summary; he may
have erred in choosing the best method of persuasion; he may have injured his argument in almost
countless other ways. In these matters a text-book

---

[1] Webster's Great Speeches, p. 23.

The Conclusion

can give only general and rather vague instruction. Each argument must be suited to the particular case in hand. There are several common errors in students' work, however, that should always be avoided and that can definitely be pointed out.

1. *An argument should not have an abrupt and jerky ending.* It is not uncommon especially in class room debate, to hear a student at the close of his discussion say, " This is my proof; I leave the decision to the judges "; or " Thus you see I have established my proposition." Such an ending can in no way be called a conclusion or a peroration.

2. *A conclusion should contain no new proof.* Violations of this principle brand an arguer as careless, and greatly weaken his argument. Proof is most convincing when arranged in its proper place and in its logical order. Furthermore, the purpose of the conclusion is to review the points that have already been established. If the arguer forgets this fact and mixes proof with summary, the audience is liable to become badly confused and not know what has been established and what has not.

3. *A conclusion should not refer to a point that has not already been established.* A careless writer or debater will sometimes state that he has

The Conclusion

proved an argument which he has not previously touched upon. Such a procedure smacks of trickery or ignorance, and is sure to be disastrous. Not only will the audience throw out that particular point, but they will be highly prejudiced against both the arguer and his argument. It is permissible for one to maintain that he has proved a point even though the proof be somewhat inadequate, but for one to refer in his conclusion to a point that he then mentions for the first time is unpardonable.

4. *A conclusion must reaffirm the proposition exactly as stated at the beginning.* Sometimes a writer, discovering at the close of his argument that he has not stuck to his subject but has proved something different, or at best has proved only a part of his subject, states as his decision a totally different proposition from that with which he started. To illustrate, a student once attempted to argue on the affirmative side of the proposition, " The United States should discontinue its protective tariff policy "; but he gave as his concluding sentence, " These facts, then, prove to you that our present tariff duties are too high." This last sentence embodied the real proposition which he had discussed, and if he had taken as his subject, " Our present tariff duties are too high," his argument would have been suc-

The Conclusion

cessful. As it was, his failure to support the proposition with which he started rendered his whole effort worthless.

A conclusion that is weaker than the proposition is commonly called a "qualifying conclusion." When one has fallen into this error there are two possible ways of removing it: one is to change the whole argument so that the conclusion will affirm the truth or falsity of the proposition; the other is to change the proposition. In a debate, of course, or whenever a subject is assigned, the latter method cannot be followed.

As a final example of what a good peroration should be, consider the following conclusion of Webster's speech, delivered in the United States Senate, on *The Presidential Veto of the United States Bank Bill*. Notice the skillful interweaving of conviction and persuasion, and remember in connection with the principle of proportion that this is the conclusion of a speech containing about 14,000 words.

"Mr. President, we have arrived at a new epoch. We are entering on experiments, with the government and the Constitution of the country, hitherto untried, and of fearful and appalling aspect. This message calls us to the contemplation of a future which little resembles the past. Its principles are at war with all that public opinion has sustained, and all which the experience of the government has sanctioned. It denies first principles; it

The Conclusion

contradicts truths, hitherto received as indisputable. It denies to the judiciary the interpretation of law, and claims to divide with Congress the power of originating statutes. It extends the grasp of executive pretension over every power of the government. But this is not all. It presents the chief magistrate of the Union in the attitude of arguing away the powers of that government over which he has been chosen to preside; and adopting for this purpose modes of reasoning which, even under the influence of all proper feeling towards high official station, it is difficult to regard as respectable. It appeals to every prejudice which may betray men into a mistaken view of their own interests, and to every passion which may lead them to disobey the impulses of their understanding. It urges all the specious topics of State rights and national encroachment against that which a great majority of the States have affirmed to be rightful, and in which all of them have acquiesced. It sows, in an unsparing manner, the seeds of jealousy and ill-will against that government of which its author is the official head. It raises a cry, that liberty is in danger, at the very moment when it puts forth claims to powers heretofore unknown and unheard of. It affects alarm for the public freedom, when nothing endangers that freedom so much as its own unparalleled pretences. This, even, is not all. It manifestly seeks to inflame the poor against the rich; it wantonly attacks whole classes of the people, for the purpose of turning against them the prejudices and the resentment of other classes. It is a state paper which finds no topic too exciting for its use, no passion to inflammable for its address and its solicitation.

Such is this message. It remains now for the people of the United States to choose between the principles here avowed and their government. These cannot subsist together. The one or the other must be rejected. If the sentiments of the message shall receive general approba-

The Conclusion

tion, the Constitution will have perished even earlier than the moment which its enemies originally allowed for the termination of its existence. It will not have survived to its fiftieth year." [1]

[1] Webster's Great Speeches, page 338.

APPENDICES

APPENDIX A

A WRITTEN ARGUMENT AND ITS BRIEF.

SHOULD IMMIGRATION BE RE-STRICTED?[1]

SIMON GREENLEAF CROSWELL

DURING recent years there has been a growing interest in plans for further checking or limiting the tide of immigration whose waves sweep in upon the United States almost daily in constantly increasing volume. Several restrictive measures are already in force: paupers, idiots, contract laborers, the Chinese, and several other classes of people are prohibited from entering our ports. The subject has been discussed in legislatures, in political meetings, from pulpits, in reform clubs, and among individuals on every hand. The reason for the interest which the subject now excites is easily found in the recent enormous increase of immigration.

The problem divides itself at the outset into two

---

[1] The North American Review, May, 1897, page 526.

Argument and Brief

SHOULD IMMIGRATION BE RE-STRICTED?

Negative Brief.

INTRODUCTION.

I. The enormous increase in immigration gives rise to a growing interest in some plan for further limiting the number of immigrants coming to the United States.

A. Paupers, idiots, contract laborers, the Chinese, and several other classes of people are already excluded.

B. The subject has been discussed in legislatures, in political meetings, from pulpits, in reform clubs, and among individuals.

II. The problem divides itself into two distinct questions :—

Argument and Brief

distinct questions: First, is it for the advantage of the United States that immigration be further checked or limited? Second, if so, in what way should the check or limit be applied?

It is evident that these questions cover two distinct fields of inquiry, the industrial and the political. Nor can the two fields be examined simultaneously, for the reasons, if there are any, from a political point of view, why immigration should be limited, would not apply to the questions viewed on its industrial side, and *vice versa*.

Taking up first the industrial question, we may assume that the entrance of the swarms of immigrants into our country represents the introduction of just so much laboring power into the country, and we may also assume as a self-evident proposition that the introduction of laboring power into an undeveloped or partially developed country is advantageous until the point is reached at which all the laborers whom the country can support have been introduced. Adam Smith says that labor is the wealth of nations. If this is true, the laborer is the direct and only primary means of acquiring wealth. The facts of the history of our country bear out this view. Beginning with the clearing of the forests, the settlements of the villages, the culti-

Argument and Brief

   A. Is it for the advantage of the United States that immigration be further checked or limited?

   B. If so, in what way should the check or limit be applied?

III. These questions must be considered, first, from the industrial point of view; and, secondly, from the political point of view.

DISCUSSION.

Immigration should not be further restricted, for

I. From an industrial point of view, the United States needs immigrants, for

   A. Without question, immigrants represent laboring power.

   B. The United States needs more laboring power, for

      1. Admittedly, the introduction of laboring power into an undeveloped or partially developed country is advantageous up to the saturation point.

         a. Adam Smith says that labor is the wealth of nations.

vation of farms, proceeding to the establishment of
the lumber industries, the cultivation of vast wheat
and corn fields, the production of cotton, the working of the coal and oil fields of Pennsylvania, the development of the mining districts of the West, cul-
minating in the varied and extensive manufactures
of the Eastern and Central States, the laborer has
been the Midas whose touch has turned all things
to gold.

There is, however, a limitation to the principle
that the introduction of laborers into a partially developed country is advantageous. A point is finally
reached which may be called the saturation point of
the country; that is, it has as many inhabitants as it
can supply with reasonably good food and clothing.
This saturation point may be reached many times in
the history of a country, for the ratio between the
food and clothing products and the population is
constantly varying. New modes of cultivation, and
the use of machinery, as well as natural causes affecting the fertility of land, which are as yet obscure, render a country at one time capable of sup-
porting a much larger number of inhabitants than
at another time. Still, there is a broad and general
truth that, time and place and kind of people being

b. The history of America has borne out this statement, for

    1′. The laborer has turned the forests, fields, and mines into wealth.

2. The United States is still under-populated, for

considered, some countries are over-populated, and some are under-populated.

We are accustomed to say that some of the countries of Europe are over-populated, and there are among us some who are beginning to say that the United States has reached the same point. This is far from being the case, and a single glance at the comparative average density of population of the principal European nations and of the United States will be sufficient to drive this idea out of any fair-minded person's head.

The most thickly settled country of modern Europe is the Netherlands, which had, in the year 1890, the very large average of three hundred and fifty-nine inhabitants per square mile of territory. Great Britain came next, with the almost equally large average of three hundred and eleven inhabitants per square mile of territory. Germany had two hundred and thirty-four and France one hundred and eighty-seven. Taking in for purposes of comparison, though not of much force in the argument, China, we find there an average population of two hundred and ninety-five inhabitants per square mile of territory. It is a question of some difficulty to decide in any specific case whether a country has reached the point of over-population. We may ad-

Argument and Brief

a. There is a smaller population to the square mile than in many European countries, for

1'. In 1890 the Netherlands had the average of three hundred and fifty-nine inhabitants to the square mile

Argument and Brief

mit that Great Britain, with its average of three hundred and eleven inhabitants per mile, is over-populated, though the conditions of life do not seem to be wholly intolerable, even to the lowest classes there.   If Great Britain is over-populated, *a fortiori* are the Netherlands, and we may even go so far as to admit that Germany, with its average of two hundred and thirty-four inhabitants per square mile, is over-populated.   But when we come to France, with its one hundred and eighty-seven inhabitants per square mile, we may pause and see what are the conditions of the French people.   So far as it is possible to judge of a people in the lump, it would seem that the population of France is not excessive for the area.   The land holdings are divided up into very small lots, but are held by a great number of people.   Mackenzie, in his history of the nineteenth century, says that nearly two-thirds of the French householders are landowners, while only one British householder in every four is an owner of land. This condition results partly from the difference in the system of inheritance of land in the two countries, but would be impossible if the country were over-populated.   Moreover, there are five millions of people in France whose possessions in land are under six acres each.

Argument and Brief

2'. Great Britain had the average
of three hundred and eleven.

3'. Germany had two hundred and
thirty-four.

4'. France had one hundred and
eighty-seven.

Argument and Brief

Taking, then, the population of France, averaging 187 per square mile, as being at least not above the normal rate of population, what do we find in comparing it with the population of the United States? We find over here vast tracts of country, amounting to nearly one-third by actual measurement, of the whole area of the United States, and including all the States west of the Missouri and Mississippi valleys (except a portion of California), having a population of less than six individuals per square mile. It would seem as if the mere statement of this fact were alone sufficient to disprove any proposition which asserts that the saturation point of population has been reached in the United States. While that immense expanse of country averages only six individuals to the square mile, there can be no reason for saying that this country is over-populated. Coming now to the more thickly settled portions of the United States, we find a large area spread out over various parts of the States having a population between seven and forty-five individuals per square mile. In a very few States, New York, Pennsylvania, Michigan, Ohio, and Indiana, the population of the whole State averages over forty-five and under ninety individuals per square mile, and the same average holds in parts of Massachusetts, Con-

Argument and Brief

5′. In about one-third of the whole area of the United States, the average is less than six.

6′. In certain more thickly settled portions the average is from seven to forty-five.

7′. In New York, Pennsylvania, Michigan, Ohio, and Indiana, the average is from forty-five to ninety.

necticut, Illinois, Kentucky, and isolated spots in the South. In a small territory, made up of parts of Massachusetts, Pennsylvania, and New Jersey, the population averages over ninety per square mile.

The contrast between these averages of population in various portions of the United States, the highest of which is about ninety individuals per mile (and that over very small portions of the area of the United States) and the average densities of the European countries, previously examined, shows how very far the United States is from complete population. This appears still more clearly when the average population of the United States taken as a whole, is considered, which is the extraordinary low figure of twenty individuals per square mile of territory. What a striking contrast! Can the most ardent advocate of the Malthusian doctrine claim that the United States already has too many inhabitants, or is in danger of having too many in the immediate future? Do we not rather need to encourage immigration, to fling wide open the gates of our country and secure as large an addition to our working force as possible?

When we come to the political aspect of the problem, however, a wholly different series of considerations present themselves. The question now is not

8'. In a small territory made up of parts of Massachusetts, Pennsylvania, and New Jersey, the average is over ninety.

9'. In the United States as a whole, the average is twenty.

II. From a political point of view, the immigrants who are arriving at our shores make good citizens, for

how many citizens, but what sort of citizens. The theory of our government is not limited to any number of people. It provides for expansion in the number of representatives in Congress in proportion to the increase in population, and increases the number of Senators as new States are formed and added to the Union. Similarly each State government has elastic provisions which enable it to cover a population of 400,000 as well as a population of 40,000. But the one critical test in determining whether or not our immigration should be limited for political reasons is the character of the people whom we are admitting to the privilege of citizenship in the United States.

In order to investigate successfully the political effect of the immigration, it is necessary, at the outset, to divide it into its constituent nationalities, so that taking up each nationality in turn, we may see what fitness it has from its previous political training in its native country for undertaking the duties of American citizenship. The disintegration of the tide of immigration into these constituent parts affords some interesting information which will be seen to have a bearing, in several directions, on the questions under consideration in this article. Taking the statistics of the year 1891 as a typical year of

Argument and Brief

A. Their previous political training has been such as to render them capable of learning how to perform the duties of American citizenship, for

recent immigration, the tide of immigration amounted in round numbers to 500,000 individuals.

The largest feeder of this enormous stream came from Germany, which sent, roughly speaking, 100,-000. But a noticeable point about this nationality is the great decrease in the number of immigrants it has sent us in the last fifteen years. In the year 1882 the total German immigration into the United States amounted to no less than 250,000, but in 1883 and 1884 there was a great decrease, and since then the average has remained in the neighborhood of 100,000. We shall see later that on the other hand, the immigration from the Latin and Slav nations of Europe, particularly Italy, Poland, and Austria, shows an enormous rate of increase in the same period, although, of course, the absolute amounts are much less than those of the German immigration.

The next largest feeder to our stream of immigration in the year 1891, the typical year of our examination, was Italy, which contributed 76,000 immigrants to our population. It is noteworthy to remark, in this connection, that Italy has more than doubled her annual rate of contributions to our people in the ten years under consideration, the immigration from her shores in 1882 being only 32,000.

Argument and Brief

1. Of the 500,000 immigrants that arrived in 1891, Germany sent approximately 100,000.

2. Italy sent 76,000.

Argument and Brief

The next largest contributor is Austria, which in 1891 furnished 71,000 new members of our community. Austria, too, has doubled her rate of contribution, sending us in 1882 only 32,000. Next come, side by side, in their offerings to our population, England and Ireland, each of which countries sends us about 50,000 new inhabitants each year, and has continued to do so for the last fifteen years. Russia, exclusive of Poland, sent 47,000 in 1891, this being three times the number which she sent in 1882, a large increase. Sweden came next with 36,000 immigrants and that country shows a woeful falling-off of nearly one-half in the ten years under consideration, for in the year 1882 it sent 64,000. Poland in 1891 sent us 27,000 immigrants, showing an enormous increase of nearly sevenfold over its contribution of 4,000 in 1882. Scotland and Norway and Denmark all send about the same number, that is, about 12,000 each; Norway showing a diminution in the decade ending 1891, from 29,000 in 1882, but the other two remaining about stationary. Switzerland in 1891 sent 6,000, a diminution from 10,000 in 1882. The Netherlands sent 5,000 in 1891, a decrease from 9,000 in 1882. France sent 6,000 and Belgium 3,000, these figures being about the same during all the years covered by our inves-

Argument and Brief

3. Austria sent 78,000.

4. England and Ireland sent 50,000
   each.
5. Russia, exclusive of Poland, sent 47,-
   000.

6. Sweden sent 36,000.

7. Poland sent 27,000.

8. Scotland, Norway, and Denmark
   sent 12,000 each.

9. Switzerland sent 6,000.

10. The Netherlands sent 5,000.
11. France sent 6,000.
12. Belgium sent 3,000.

tigation. I have left out of account the only other important factor in our immigration in the ten years considered, namely, China, because the door was shut in its face with considerable emphasis in 1883, and the immigration from China to the Western States, which in 1882 amounted to 40,000 fell in 1883 to 8,000, and in 1884 to 279 individuals, and may, therefore, be neglected at the present time.

Now, an examination of the political institutions in the countries from which these immigrants come would show that in almost no case, that of Russia and Poland alone excepted, are the elements of representative government wholly unknown to the common people. In most of these countries, some form of popular government has, either wholly or partially, gained a footing, with the inevitable result of accustoming people more or less to representative institutions. Yet the short time that this has been the case in many of the countries which pour half or over of the total flood of immigration into the United States, and the long centuries of despotism which preceded this partial and recent enlightenment, make it painfully evident that there can be, in the large part of our immigrants, little knowledge of the republican form of government, and little inherited aptitude for such government. It would at

13. Except in Russia and Poland, the elements of representative government are not wholly unknown to these people, for

    a. In most of these countries some form of popular government has either wholly or partially gained a footing.

first seem as if the results of such immigration must be disastrous to our country.

And yet the situation is not so hopeless. There is nothing mysterious, or even very complicated, about republican institutions. A little time, a little study, a little experience with the practical workings of elections, is sufficient to convey to any person of ordinary intelligence as much familiarity with these matters as is necessary for the intelligent appreciation of their objects and purposes. Nor is the material out of which the prospective citizen is to be made wholly unfitted for its purpose. To be sure, the Latin races, the Slavs, Hungarians, Poles, and others have no inherited aptitude, nor if we may judge from the history of the races, any inherent capacity for self-government and free institutions, but, as I have before said, in almost every case they have had in their own country a partial training in the forms of representative government. All that is needed is to amalgamate this heterogeneous mass, to fuse its elements in the heat and glow of our national life, until, formed in the mould of everyday experience, each one shall possess the characteristic features of what we believe to be the highest type of human development which the world has seen, the American citizen.

Argument and Brief

B. The duties of the American citizen are not
   hard to learn, for
   1. Republican institutions are not very
      complicated.

Argument and Brief

The process of acquiring American citizenship is regulated by acts of Congress. It is a simple process. Practically all that is required is a continuous residence of five years in the States, and one year in the special State in which citizenship is applied for, and the declaration of intention to become a citizen may be made immediately upon landing. This last point will be seen later to be very important.

Citizenship in the United States, however, under the act of Congress, does not carry with it the right to vote. This right is entirely a matter of State regulation, and the Constitution or statutes of each State settle who shall have the right to vote in its elections. The underlying idea of the whole system is universal male suffrage, and the franchise is granted (after a certain residence, which will be discussed later) with only certain general limitations of obvious utility, such as that the voter must be twenty-one years of age, that he must not be an idiot or insane, and generally, that he must not have been convicted of any felony or infamous crime, although in many States a pardon, or the serving of a sentence, will restore a felon to his civil rights. In a few of the States paupers are also excluded from voting. With the question of woman suffrage we have nothing to do, as its settlement, one way or the

Argument and Brief

C. The political ignorance of the immigrant can be remedied, for

    1. Before extending immigrants the franchise, States can insist on requirements that will secure some preliminary training in free political institutions, since

        a. The right to vote is entirely a matter of State regulation, for

            1'. Citizenship, which is regulated by Congress, does not carry with it the franchise.

other, does not affect the subject we are discussing.

The important qualification, however, in relation to the subjects which we are discussing, is that which requires residence in the State previous to the exercise of the franchise. And on this point the States may be divided into two great classes. One class allows no one to vote who is not, under the laws of Congress, a citizen of the United States, either native or naturalized. As we have seen that five years' residence is a requisite to United States citizenship, these States, therefore, require five years' residence as a prerequisite to acquiring the right to vote. These States are California, Connecticut, Georgia, Illinois, Iowa, Kentucky, Maine, Maryland, Massachusetts, Michigan, Montana, Nevada, New Jersey, New York, Ohio, Pennsylvania, Rhode Island, South Carolina, Tennessee, Vermont, Virginia, and Washington. This requirement is admirably calculated to secure that preliminary training in the practical working of our institutions which must be necessary to most of the immigrants before they can intelligently exercise the rights which are conferred upon them by American citizenship and we cannot but admire the sagacity and judiciousness of those who framed our naturalization laws in selecting this period of time for

Argument and Brief

b. Already twenty-two States allow
    no one to vote who has not been
    in the United States at least five
    years.

Argument and Brief

the pupilage of the intending citizen. The period is long enough even for one who is engrossed in the cares of earning a support for himself and his family, amid all the excitement and novelty of a changed residence, to acquire in the five succeeding annual elections a sufficient knowledge of republican government for all practical purpose. To delay him longer in the exercise of his political rights would be an injustice; to admit him to them sooner would be an imprudence.

There are in a few States other qualifications required of a voter. The most important of these is the educational qualification, which exists only in Connecticut and Massachusetts. In neither of these is it very severe. In Connecticut the voter must be able to read any article in the State Constitution, and any section of the statutes. In Massachusetts he must be able to read the Constitution and to write his name. Too much praise can hardly be given to these requirements. The whole edifice of our national life is founded upon education, and to this potent factor must we look for many of the improvements necessary to the proper development of our national life.

In quite a number of States a pecuniary qualification exists in the shape of the payment of some tax,

Argument and Brief

c. **Massachusetts and Connecticut have an educational test.**

345

generally a poll tax, within two years previous to the date of the election. This requirement does not seem to be so germane to the spirit of our institutions as the other. The great present danger of our country is the danger of becoming a plutocracy, and while there is no doubt that a widespread interest in property develops stability of institutions, yet there is also great danger of capital obtaining so firm and strong a hold upon political institutions as to crush out the life of free government and to convert the national government into a species of close corporation, in which the relative wealth of the parties alone controls. This qualification is found in Delaware, Florida, Georgia, Mississippi, Nevada, Pennsylvania, Tennessee, and Texas.

We have now examined with some thoroughness the component parts of the tide of immigration as it arrives at our shores; we have seen what nationalities go to make up the grand total and what previous training they have had in the political institutions of their native countries to fit them for American citizenship, and what additional requirements are imposed upon them by our statutes before they can participate in voting and government in this country. What are the conclusions to which the view of these facts brings us? They seem to

d. Eight States insist on a pecuniary
qualification.

me to be these: first, that the growth of immigration is a desirable thing for this country from an industrial point of view; second, that the immigrants who arrive at our shores are for the most part good material out of which to make American citizens. Applying these conclusions to the questions which were stated at the outset of this article; first, is it for the advantage of the United States that immigration should be checked or limited? second, if so, in what way should the check or limit be applied? the answer would be that no further check or limit should be applied, but that a check should be placed upon the exercise of the franchise by immigrants in all States by requiring a residence of five years in this country before they can vote, and by also requiring some moderate educational test.

With these safeguards established we might look without any serious apprehension upon the increase of our population. The founders of our state moulded the outlines of its form in large and noble lines. The skeleton has grown and clothed itself with flesh with almost incredible rapidity in the hundred years of its existence. But it is still young. We should avoid any measures which would stunt or deform its growth and should allow it to develop freely and generously till the full-grown American

Argument and Brief

The following points have been proved:—

I. The growth of immigration is a desirable thing for this country from an industrial point of view.

II. The immigrants who arrive at our shores are for the most part good material out of which to make American citizens.

Therefore, no further check or limit should be applied to immigration.

nation stands forth pre-eminent among the nations of the earth, in size, as well as in character and organization, and man's last experiment in government is clearly seen to be an unequivocal success.

APPENDIX B

A LIST OF PROPOSITIONS.

1. The United States army should be greatly enlarged.

2. Japan was justified in waging war against Russia.

3. A formal alliance between the United States and Great Britain for the protection and advancement of their common interests would be expedient.

4. Military tactics should be taught in the public schools.

5. The United States navy should be greatly enlarged.

6. The aggressions of England in South Africa are justifiable.

7. The nations of Europe should combine to bring about drastic reforms in the Congo Free State.

8. Ireland should be granted home rule.

9. Japanese control will promote the political and

Propositions

economic interests of Corea more than would Russian control.

10. Armed intervention on the part of any nation to collect private claims against any other nation is not justifiable.

11. The annexation of Canada by treaty with Great Britain would be economically advantageous to the United States.

12. The United States should establish commercial reciprocity with Canada.

13. The United States should maintain a system of subsidies for the protection of American merchant marine.

14. Congress should have decided in favor of a sea-level canal at Panama.

15. Woman suffrage should be adopted by an amendment to the Constitution.

16. The practice of relieving financial stringency by temporary deposits of United States Treasury funds in selected banks should be discontinued.

17. Labor unions are detrimental to the best interests of the workingman.

18. Free trade should be established between the United States and the Philippine Islands.

19. State boards of arbitration, with compulsory

Propositions

powers, should be appointed to settle disputes between employers and employees.

20. The United States should discontinue the protective tariff policy.

21. The Federal government should own and operate the interstate railroads within its borders.

22. Railroad pooling should be legalized.

23. The tax on the issues of state banks should be repealed.

24. The United States should adopt one-cent postage.

25. American municipalities should own and operate their street-car systems.

26. The President of the United States should be elected for a term of six years and be ineligible for re-election.

27. The President of the United States should be elected by popular vote.

28. Ex-Presidents of the United States should be Senators-at-large for life.

29. United States Senators should be elected by popular vote.

30. The powers of the Speaker of the House of Representatives should be restricted.

31. The United States should institute a system of responsible cabinet government.

353

Propositions

32. Judges should be elected by direct vote of the people.

33. All cities in the State of ——, having at least ten thousand inhabitants should adopt the Des Moines plan of government.

34. The right of suffrage should be limited by an educational test.

35. The State of —— should adopt the initiative and referendum system of government.

36. Congress should repeal the Fifteenth Amendment.

37. Members of State legislatures should be forbidden by law to accept free passes on any railroads.

38. Corporations engaged in interstate commerce should be required to take out a Federal license.

39. Women who pay taxes should be permitted to vote at municipal elections.

40. The annexation of Cuba to the United States would be for the best interests of Cuba.

41. The United States should grant full citizenship to the people of Porto Rico.

42. The United States should establish an old age-pension system similar to the one in operation in Germany.

43. Political union with Cuba would be for the advantage of the United States.

Propositions

44. The United States should permanently retain the Philippines.

45. The House of Representatives should elect its standing committees.

46. The white citizens of the Southern States are justified in maintaining their political supremacy.

47. Congress should prohibit corporate contributions to political campaign funds.

48. The present powers of courts to grant injunctions should be curtailed.

49. In all criminal cases three-fourths of a jury should be competent to render a verdict.

50. The United States government is treating the Indians unjustly.

51. Capital punishment should be abolished.

52. Education should be compulsory to the age of sixteen.

53. The fully elective system of studies should be introduced into all colleges.

54. College students receiving an average daily grade of eighty-five per cent. in a subject should be excused from final examination in that subject.

55. Class rushes should be abolished at —— College.

56. Hazing should be abolished at all colleges.

Propositions

57. Freshmen should be debarred from intercollegiate athletic contests.

58. Athletics, as conducted at present, are detrimental to —— College.

59. The Federal government should maintain a college for the education of men for the diplomatic and consular service.

60. A large city affords a better location for a college than does the country.

61. The "honor system" should prevail at —— College.

62. American universities should admit women on equal terms with men.

63. American colleges should admit students only on examination.

64. American colleges should confer the degree of Bachelor of Arts in three years.

65. Public schools should not furnish free textbooks.

66. Secret societies should not exist in public high schools.

67. The education of the American negro should be industrial rather than liberal.

68. For the average student, the small college is preferable to the large college.

356

Propositions

69. American colleges should adopt the recommendations of the Simplified Spelling Board.

70. For the United States, the type of the German university is preferable to the type of the American university.

71. Fraternities are undesirable in colleges.

72. The United States Army canteen should be restored.

73. There should be national laws governing marriage and divorce.

74. High License is preferable to Prohibition.

75. The Federal government should take action to prevent children under the age of fourteen from working in mines and factories.

76. The elimination of private profits offers the best solution of the liquor problem.

77. Employers are justified in refusing recognition to labor unions.

78. The United States should grant permanent copyright.

79. The Chinese should be excluded from the Philippines.

80. States should prohibit vivisection involving great pain.

81. The United States should establish a parcels post.

Propositions

82. The United States should establish a postal savings bank.

83. The veto power of the House of Lords should be annulled.

84. Abdul Hamid was unjustly deposed.

85. The present laws relating to Chinese immigration should be amended to include the Japanese.

86. The United States should admit the Chinese on equal terms with other immigrants.

87. Further centralization in the power of the Federal government is contrary to the best interests of the United States.

88. The present tendency of government conservation of natural resources is contrary to the best interests of the United States.

89. Commercial reciprocity between the United States and Brazil would benefit the United States.

90. At present the United States should maintain no navy yard on the Gulf Coast.

91. The United States should admit all raw materials free of duty.

92. The United States should admit sugar free of duty.

93. The date of the Presidential inauguration should be changed.

94. Postmasters should be elected by popular vote.

Propositions

95. All cities in the United States should establish and enforce a curfew law.

96. The three term system is preferable to the semester system at —— College.

97. The products of prison labor should not be allowed to compete in the open market.

98. New York City should establish a dramatic censorship.

99. Convicts should not be farmed out to private contractors.

100. The State of —— should establish a property qualification for voting.

INDEX

Index

Index